POEMS.

POEMS

BY

THOMAS WILLIAM PARSONS.

BOSTON:
TICKNOR AND FIELDS.
M DCCC LIV.

Stereotyped by
HOBART & ROBBINS,
NEW ENGLAND TYPE AND STEREOTYPE FOUNDRY,
BOSTON.

TO

JOHN C. WARREN, M. D.,

EMERITUS PROFESSOR OF ANATOMY AND SURGERY

IN THE UNIVERSITY AT CAMBRIDGE,

ETC. ETC. ETC.

These Poems are Inscribed,

IN TOKEN OF SINCERE LOVE AND REGARD,

AND OF GRATITUDE

FOR HIS CONSTANT FRIENDSHIP.

MAY 1, 1854.

CONTENTS.

LETTERS.

MISCELLANEOUS.

LETTERS.

PREFACE TO THE LETTERS.

Ten years and more! — it seems a weary time
Since first these fancies took their shape of rhyme;
And some who praised, and many more that read
The trifling lines, are written with the dead:
Why, then, recall them? Mentor says 't is best,
Or some dear friend may, after I 'm at rest;
Or, fearful thought! should Bavius find them out,
And clap 'em in that volume he 's about,
So my boy-verses might confront my age,
And cry "Thus did'st thou!" from his tell-tale page!
What was their drift? — A whim, without a plan,
To feign myself a wandering Englishman:
To imagine how he felt, and what he thought;
How *we* had felt, perchance, if English taught:
Had we at Harrow or at Eton learned
That fine freemasonry that is not earned
By bookish toil in colleges at home,
Nor all the schools from Gottingen to Rome:
Something fastidious, — call it, if you will,
Insular pride, — but something genial still;
Something satirical, — yet common sense, —
That sees through pedantry, puts down pretence,
Knows its own nonsense, and forgiveth yours,
Calls folly by its name — and yet endures:

Good-humored wisdom, that can read the lie
Of the false world, nor be enraged thereby,
But keep its temper and its truth unmoved,
Though boobies triumph, and the quack 's approved.
But even ourselves may come to this at last
And rest content, not proud, with what is past;
Our world shall grow a less distracting scene,
And life, less busy, wear a gentler mien;
Then, too, perchance, in countries yet unclaimed
(If such there be), by rivers yet unnamed,
Where the brooks fall to the Pacific's rest,
And the sun rises in —— what *was* the West,
To many a spirit full of zeal and young,
Whose mother speech is ours and Shakspeare's tongue,
Such as to us — a consecrated stream —
Isis hath been, our little Charles may seem!
In Harvard's names, that now so humbly sound,
St. John's and Pembroke may by them be found,
And what old England is to you and me,
Such may New England to Nebraska be!

EPISTLE TO SAMUEL ROGERS, LONDON.

NESTOR of Britain's lyre! — 't is Byron's phrase —
Or Midas! (nay, I mean you no dispraise)
Midas! I say, since, whether you indite
Poems or prose, or — "payable at sight,"
With bards and bankers equally enrolled,
Whate'er you touch turns wondrously to gold;
May these rude lines, however lamely wrought,
Bring back the pilgrim to your kindly thought;
Thine was the last of many a parting word
Which my sad ear, on leaving England, heard;
Now just, it seems, arrived this side the sea,
My first epistle I address to thee.

Some value, sure, a thousand leagues may lend
To verse as dull as mild Reviews commend;
Distance and Time are marvellous magicians,
Distance gives fame — and sometimes five editions;
So common toys, by Canton's turners made,
Are marked "five pounds" in Burlington Arcade;
So may the farness of Manhattan give
At least a fortnight for my rhymes to live;
The long, salt seasoning of the Atlantic brine
Spins out the death-pangs of the weakest line.
And, O, remember, venerable SAM!
I rove not now by Thamis or the Cam;

Hesperia's muse is but a lagging bird,
By whose low flight small rivalry is stirred;
On ostrich wings her dull career is driven,—
Half tied to earth, half hopping up to heaven,—
For seldom here has genius found in art
Spontaneous utterance for a flowing heart,
Or sought by night, in forest or in glen,
The tongue of angels for the thoughts of men;
No willows planted by a poet's hand
Grace wild Weehawken, like the Twick'nham strand;
If chance a laurel spring by Hudson's bank,
It scarce grows beautiful, but only rank;
For why? Apollo's few and feeble scholars
Ply their dry tasks for dinners or for dollars!
But plume now — plume thy Fancy's willing pinion,
Behold me here in JONATHAN'S dominion;
Snug in the shelter of that savory hell,
That marble Malebolge — "HOLT'S hotel;"
Where, forced by crowds from each genteeler house,
I take, at one! some canvas-back and grouse;
With boors from Buffalo in "velvet vests,"
Sit the most silent of the ravenous guests;
Watch their huge hunger with a wondering eye,
Remember you and Holland House, and sigh.

Perchance you marvel at my long delay
Amid the pigs and liveries of Broadway;
Yet have I strayed (it 's over, to my joy!)
Far as the savage tribes of Illinois;
Scarce had I trod the threshold of the land,
When strong disgust, too potent to withstand,

Drove me, distracted with commercial cant,
And tap-room statesmen's never-ending rant,
To seek beyond the Alleghany's range
Some race whose earth was not one vast exchange;
Some sacred scene where Nature was not made
The drudge and slattern of usurping Trade.
Swift on the wings of water and of fire
I dashed through forests, to my heart's desire;
From fog and snow to flowers and sunshine went,
Surveyed the swamps—and hastened back content;
For, spite of pigs, the truth must be confessed,
Vile as this town is—'t is the country's best!
Here, at the least, our mother-tongue is spoken;
Here all the bell-strings are not always broken;
Here English looks and English manners bear,
At times, the Briton back to Berkeley-square.
Here, too, my friend, some gentle spirits dwell,
Who deign to know me—even in Holt's hotel.

They grossly err this thrifty race who call
A youthful nation;—"youthful?"—not at all!
What though some trace of the barbarian state
Betrays at times the newness of their date?
What though their dwellings rose but yesterday?
The mind, the nature of the land, is gray.
Old Europe holds not in its oldest nook
A race less juvenile in thought and look;
There seems no childhood here, no child-like joy;
Since first I landed I 've not seen a boy;
For all the children in their aspect wear
The lines of business and corrosive care;

Each babe, as soon as babyhood is past,
Is a grown man, and withers just as fast.
O, my dear England! best of lands! God bless you!
Though taxes, bishops, fogs and beer, oppress you,
Still, as of old, a jocund little isle,
Still once a year, at least, allowed a smile;
When, spite of virtue, cakes and ale abound,
And laughter rings, and glasses clink around:
Nor quite extinct is that robust old race
(Autumn's last roses blooming on their face),
Whom, spite of silver hairs and trembling knees,
At Christmas-time a pantomime can please.

Ere yet my glance anatomized aright
The insect race that fluttered in my sight,
Oft as the mote-like myriads of Broadway
I scanned, their trim and bearing to survey,
Almost at each third passenger I saw,
Scarce could my lip repress a rising "pshaw!"
And oft this line was running in my brain,
"Was ever nation like Sienna's vain!"
Surely, quoth I, could emptiness and froth,
And the poor pride of superfinest cloth,
Make more ridiculous a thing than these
Pert, whiskered, insolent Manhattanese?
But soon I found how poor a patriot I,—
'T was mine own countrymen I saw go by!
O, altered race! with hair upon your chins,
Spaniards in strut and Frenchmen in your grins;
The "snob" and shop-keeper but ill concealed
By boots of Paris, bright and brazen-heeled,

Made up of coxcomb, pugilist and sot,—
Are ye true Englishmen? I know ye not!

With what fierce air, how lion-like a swell,
They pace the pavement of the grand hotel;
On each new guest with regal stare look down,
Or "strike him dead with a victorious frown"!
These are the fools whom I for natives took,
Ere I could read their nation in their look;
Now wiser grown, I recognize each ass
For a true bit of Birmingham's own brass.
Some are third cousins of the penny press,
Skilful a piquant paragraph to dress;
Some in their veins a dash patrician boast,—
Them Stültz has banished from their native coast;
There stalks a lecturer, bearing in his mien
More glories than he bought at Aberdeen;
These are tragedians,—wandering stars,—and those
Manchester men—deep-read in calicos!

Ye reverend gods, who guard the household flame!
Lares, Penates,—whatsoe'er your name,—
What dire subversion of your sway divine
Lets loose all cockneydom to tempt the brine?
Why from the counter and the club-room so
Flock the spruce trader and the Bond-street beau?
Why should the lordling and the Marquis come?
And many a snug possessor of a plum,
Quitting his burrow on the 'Ampstead road,
With wife and trunks be flying all abroad?
Is it in rivers and in rocks to find
Some new sensation for a barren mind?

From kindred manners, doctrines, men and sects,
To learn a lesson of their own defects?
Or with rapt eye on cataracts to look?
No, their sole passion is — to spawn a book.
Hence this poor land so scribbled o'er has been,
'T is like a window in some country inn,
Where every dolt has chronicled his folly,
His fit of head-ache or of melancholy;
With memorandums of his mutton oft,
And how his bed was hard, his butter soft;
How some John Tomson, on a rainy day,
Found naught to eat — but very much to pay,
And how said Tomson wished himself away.

Oft at your board, at that refined repast
Where London's lions break their morning fast,
To "nights and suppers of the gods" preferring
Green tea and temperance, with a toast and herring;
Oft have you said, perchance in jesting mood,
You too might venture o'er the foamy flood;
Might take the whim, some sweet September day,
When scarce a cat in Portland-place will stay;
When all the town, beyond the reach of duns,
Is out of town, with horses, dogs and guns;
To shut your books, and take your annual rest
In the green bosom of the woody west:
Where, by some river, with an Indian name,
Your living ears might antedate your fame;
In "Thebes" or "Troy" your living eyes admire
Your plaster bust with laurel and with lyre;
See your sweet self, biography and all,
In Philadelphia blazoned on a wall;

Or, cheaply printed for the southern trade,
As far as Arkansas to be conveyed,
Where Peck, the "Pindar of the Sucker State,"
May call you, in his classic way, "*first rate.*"
Charming! to find in Geneseo's vale
Some damsel sighing o'er GINEVRA's tale!
To say the lines that pleased the Thames before
By the wild music of Niagara's roar,
And thus to "Memory's Pleasures" add one more.

Yet, Nestor, pause! quit not your home for this
Imperfect picture of an author's bliss:
Let Dickens tell you how this age of steam
Reduces poesy to weight and ream,
Retails cheap genius, brings the Muses down,
And turns Parnassus to a trading town.
Yes, the fine flashes of instinctive thought,
In silver lines and golden periods wrought;
In some blest mood of happy Fancy struck
From flinty Labor, by a touch of Luck;
The tender shoots that bourgeon from the brain,
To live and blossom on the page again;
The pretty nurslings Meditation rears,
Warmed at the hearth-stone of the heart for years,
Soon as they touch this equalizing coast,
Doff the gay "primer" and the folio-post;
Dressed in a suit of macerated rags,
Cast off by Russia's beggarmen and hags,
On huckster stalls the darling dreams must lie,
Tempting the pence from every idler by.
Ah, Nestor! how 't would gall thee to behold
Perchance all "Italy" for ninepence sold!

How would'st thou shame to recognize thyself
To common crockery turned from MOXON's delph;
In mammoth quartos, decked with wooden cuts,
Meanly displayed 'mid candies, cake and nuts;
Thumbed by coarse hands that paw before they choose,
Whether a poem — or a pair of shoes!

O! tell ANACREON, when he quits his groves
To sip with you the Mocha that he loves,
That where Ohio wears the hues of wine,
From slaughtered tribes of Cincinnatian swine,
Down by the water, near the "Pork Dépôt,"
Where drays and steamboats roar, spit, hiss and blow,
Amid the vulgar sights that throng the strand,
I saw disconsolate a PERI stand!
Hard by was ALCIPHRON, — both pale, both lean,—
While PAUL DE KOCK profanely sneaked between;
Around lay many an imp of modern song,
Here "Lays of Rome," and here "Miss LUCY LONG."
Lo! from the wharf a rugged boatman comes,
To pick a few cheap literary crumbs;
A greasy, poor, but free, enlightened man,
A foe of kings, a plain republican:
With sapient eye he views the lettered store,
Spells the strange names, and scans the pictures o'er;
Nibbling a bit of this, a bit of that,
His purchase made, he rams it in his hat;
Three-pence the freeman gave for one thin book,
Three-pence, ANACREON, for thy "Lalla Rookh!"

Tell proud LOCHIEL, when you encounter next,
How oft his Highland temper would be vexed

To see that verse, whose labor made him lean,
Stuck in the chinks of some low magazine;
Hid, like a Warsaw palace, built 'mid hovels,
Amid ten chapters of ten nauseous novels;
Robbed of the little honor of a volume,
Crammed in to fill some paper's final column;
And so perchance to have a tailor send
His garments home in verse himself had penned!
Or, worst of all, his mangled odes peruse,
Trimmed in the fashion of the Bowery muse;
For each smart editor is careful here
To clip his matter to his reader's ear;
And oft, more room to make for better men,
Bids "BLAKE and mighty NELSON" fall again.
So patriotic managers are wont
To strike out all that might free ears affront;
And, heedless how their change the measure mars,
In British plays lug in their "stripes and stars."

"Good Heavens!" methinks I hear my Samuel cry,
"With what a low, derogatory eye
You view the beautiful, primeval shore
Where first-born forests guard the torrent's roar!
What! is there nothing in that lovely land,
Mid all that 's fair, and excellent, and grand,
Nothing more worthy of a poet's pen
Than sots and rogues and bastard Englishmen?"
Patience, philosopher! as yet I dwell
In the dull echoes of a tavern-bell;
My inspiration is not born of rocks,
Nor meads, nor mountains white with snowy flocks;

'T is not Niagara thrills me — but the noise
Of drays and ferry-boats and bawling boys;
And scarce the day one quiet hour affords
To fit my fancies with harmonious words;
Yet oft at evening, when the moon is up,
When trees on dew — and men on slumber sup,
Along the gas-lit rampart of the bay,
In rhymeful mood, as undisturbed I stray,
Awhile my present "whereabout" I lose,
And on my loved ones, o'er the water, muse.
Sometimes lulled ocean heaves an orient sigh,
Which brings our terrace and its roses nigh;
While each Æolian murmur of the sea
Seems whispering fragrantly of home and thee;
But something soon dispels the pleasing dream,
The fire-fly's flash, the night-hawk's whistling scream,
Or katydid, complaining in the dark,
Or other sound unheard in Regent's Park.
For wheresoe'er by night or noon I tread,
Thought guides me still, like Ariadne's thread,
Through shops and crowds and placard-pasted walls,
Till on my brain Sleep's filmy finger falls,
And cuts the filament, with gentle knife,
That leads me through this labyrinth of life.
I feel it now, — the power of the dull god; —
The verse imperfect halts: Samuel, I nod:
'T is late, — o'er Caurus hangs the northern car!
My page is out — and so is your cigar.

EPISTLE TO CHARLES KEMBLE, LONDON.

Good Cassio, Charles, Mercutio, Benedick
(Of all your names I scarce know which to pick),
Be not alarmed; this comes not from a dun,
Nor any scheming, transatlantic Bunn,
Tempting with golden hopes your waning years,
Like "certain stars shot madly from their spheres,"
Like Matthews or old Dowton, to expose
The shank all shrunken from its youthful hose;
So boldly read, howe'er it make you sigh,—
Nor manager nor creditor am I.

Not long ago, conversing at the Club
Which Londoners with "Garrick's" title dub,
We both confessed, and each with equal grief,
That poor Melpomene was past relief;
So many symptoms of her dotage shows
This nineteenth century of steam and prose.
Nor in herself, said you, entirely lies
The incurable complaint whereof she dies;
'T is not alone that play-wrights are too poor
For gods, or men, or columns, to endure; *
Nor that all players in a mould are cast,
Every new Roscius aping still the last;

* By the word "columnæ," Horace (though Bentley knew it not) evidently meant the columns of the Roman newspapers.

Nor yet that taste's too delicate excess
Demands perfection and despises less;
But mere indifference, that worst disease,
From bard and actor takes all power to please.
How strive to please? when all their friends that were
To empty benches empty sounds prefer;
And seek, like bees attracted by a gong,
The fairy-land of tip-toe and of song;
Whether a voice of more than earthly strain
Be newly sent by Danube or the Seine,
Or some aërial, thistle-downy thing
Float from La Scala on a zephyr's wing.
Say, might a SIDDONS, conjured from the tomb,
Again the scene of her renown illume,
Could her high art (ay, even at half price)
The crowd from "La Sonnambula" entice?
No; dance and song, the Drama's deadly plagues,
RUBINI'S notes, and ELLSLER'S heavenly legs,
Would nightly still bring amateurs in flocks,
To watch the "bravos" of the royal box.

While thus, between our walnuts and our wine,
We mourned with sighs your mistress's decline,
You half indulged the fond imagination,
That what seemed death was but her *emigration.*
Perhaps, quoth you, — and 't was a bold "perhaps," —
Ere many years of exile shall elapse,
The wandering maid may find in foreign lands
More loving hearts and hospitable hands.
Perchance her feet, with furry buskins graced,
May shuddering walk the cold Canadian waste,

And rest contented with a bleak repose
In shrubless climes of never-thawing snows.
Yes, in those woods that gird the northern lakes,
Pathless, as yet, and wild with shaggy brakes,
Or in the rank savannas of the south,
Or sea-like prairies near Missouri's mouth,
Fate may conduct her to some sacred spot,
Where to resume her sceptre and to — squat.
Some happier settlement and simpler race,
Where, though her worship lack its ancient grace,
New days may dawn, like those of royal BESS,
And every state its Avon shall possess;
Where, though in marshes resonant with frogs,
And rudely housed in temples built of logs,
The nymph, regenerate in her classic robe,
May see revived the "Fortune" and the "Globe."

Delightful dream! delightful as untrue;
Poor DRAMA! this was no domain for you.
Here never shall return that early time
When the fresh heart can vulgar life sublime,
And all the prose of our existence change
By magic power to something rich and strange
Not here, among this bargain-making tribe,
Whose tricks the Muse would sicken to describe,
Shall the dull genius of a barren age
Bring an "all-hallow'n summer" of the Stage.

Beyond that cape which mortals christen Cod,
Where drifted sand-heaps choke the scanty sod,
Round the steep shore a crooked city clings,
Sworn foe to queens, it seems, as well as kings.

On three steep hills it soars, as Rome on seven,
To claim a near relationship with heaven.
Fit home for saints! the very name it bears
A kind of sacred origin declares;
Borrowed, I find, by hunting records o'er,
From one Botolfo, canonized of yore,*
Whom bards have left nor epitaph nor verse on,
Though in his day, sans doubt, a decent person:
This town, in olden times of stake and flame,
A famous nest of Puritans became;
Sad, rigid souls, who hated as they ought
The carnal arms wherewith the devil fought;
Dancing and dicing, music, and whate'er
Spreads for humanity the pleasing snare.
Stage-plays, especially, their hearts abhorred,
Holding the muses hateful to the Lord,
Save when old Sternhold and his brother bard
Oped their hoarse throats, and strained an anthem hard.

From that angelic race of perfect men
(Sure, seraphs never trod the world till then!)
Descends the race to whom the sway is given
Of the world's morals by confiding Heaven.
These of each virtue know the market price,
And shrewdly count the cost of every vice;
So, to their prudent adage faithful still,
Are honest more from policy than will,
As if with Heaven a bargain they had made
To practise goodness — and to be well paid.
They too, devoutly as their fathers did,
Sin, sack and sugar, equally forbid;

* The name of Boston, in Lincolnshire, is said to be derived from St. Botolph — quasi Botolph's town.

Holding each hour unpardonably spent
Which on the ledger leaves no monument;
While oft they read, with small, but pious wit,
The inscription o'er the play-house portals writ,
In a bad sense — " *The entrance to the Pit.*"

Once these Botolphians, when their boards you trod,
Received you almost as a demi-god;
Rushed to the teeming rows in frantic swarms,
And rained applauses, not in showers, but storms.
But should you now their fickle welcome ask,
Faint shouts would greet the veteran of the mask;
And, ah! what anguish would it be to search
For your old play-house in a bastard church!
To find the dome wherein your hour you strutted
Altered and maimed, and circumcised and gutted;
Become in truth, all metaphor to drop,
A mongrel thing — half chapel and half shop!
Long had the augur and the priest foretold
The sad reverse they doomed it to behold;
Long had the school-boy, as he passed it by,
And maiden, viewed it with presaging eye;
Oft had the wealthy deacon with a frown
Glared on the pile he longed to batter down,
And reckoned oft, with sanctimonious air,
What rents 't would fetch, if purified with prayer; *

* At the opening of the "Tremont Temple," in Boston (1843), the new proprietors chanted what they called a "Purification Hymn," of which we give one stanza:

"Satan has here held empire long —
A blighting curse, a cruel reign:
By mimic scenes, and mirth and song,
Alluring souls to endless pain."

While through the green-room whispered rumors went,
That heaven and earth were on its ruin bent.

Too just a fear! The vision long foreseen
Has come at last; behold the fallen queen!
The queen of passion, stript of all her pride,
Discrowned, indignant from her temple glide.
With draggling robe, slip-shod, her buskin loose,
She flies a sordid people's cold abuse;
Summons her sister, who forbears to smile,
And leaves to rats the desecrated pile,
Which dogs and nags already had begun,
Unless by blows and hunger driven, to shun:
For well-bred curs and steeds genteel contemn
A stage which Taste had sunk too low for them;
Whereon the town had seen, without remorse,
A herd of bisons! and a hairless horse!

Behind the two chief mourners of the band
A sad procession follows, hand in hand;
Heroes un-heroed, most unknightly knights,
Wand-broken fairies, disenchanted sprites;
Dukes no more ducal, even on the bill,
Milk-livered murderers too ill-fed to kill;
Mild-looking demons that a babe might daunt,
Witches and ghosts most naturally gaunt;
Lovers made pale by keener pangs than love's,
Unspangled princesses with greasy gloves;
Wits very witless — grave comedians mute,
And silent sons of violin and flute.

After these down-looked leaders of the show,
Who creep, like Trajan's Dacians, wan and slow,

Comes a long train of underlings that bear
Imperial robes that kings no more may wear;
With truncheons, helmets, thunderbolts and casks
Of snow and lightning — bucklers, foils and masks.

As toward the steep of Capitolian Jove
When chiefs victorious through the rabble strove,
With all their conquests in their trophies told,
And every battle marked with plundered gold, —
When the whole glory of the war rolled by,
And gaping Rome seemed all one mighty eye, —
Behind the living captives came the dead,
Poor noseless gods, and some without a head,
With pictures, ivory images and plumes,
And priceless tapestry from palace looms;
Even such, although Night's alchemy no more
The crinkling tinsel turns to precious ore,
Appears the pomp of this discarded race,
As heaped with spoil they quit their ancient place,
Bearing their Lares with them as they go —
Two dusty statues, and a bust or so —
With mail which once a Harry Fifth had on,
Triumphal cars with all the triumph gone;
Goblets of tin mixed up with Yorick's bones,
Bags made of togas — barrows formed of thrones
Whereon the majesty of Denmark sat;
Othello's handkerchief in Wolsey's hat!
Swords hacked at Bosworth, fasces, guns and spears,
Rusted with blood before, and now with tears.

Enough of this: kind prompter, touch the bell!
Children of mirth and midnight, fare ye well!

The vision melts away, — the motley crowd
Is veiled by Prospero in a passing cloud;
Like his dissolving pageantry they fade,
The vapory stuff whereof our dreams are made;
No more malignant winter to beguile,
Nor start the maiden's tear, the judge's smile;
Save when some annalist, like me, recalls
The ancient fame of those degraded walls;
Or till an age less hateful to the Muse
To their old shape restore the " anxious pews "

EPISTLE TO EDWARD MOXON, PUBLISHER, LONDON.

The fiery bark that brought your missives o'er
Brought the sad news that Murray was no more.
From Staten Island, where I chanced to stray,
I marked the monster puffing up the bay,
And guessed (already have I learned to *guess*),
From her black look, she told of some distress.
Tidings of gloom her sable pennon spoke,
And the long train of her funereal smoke;
And soon the bulletins revealed the grief:
"John Murray 's dead! of booksellers the chief!"

In all the dread events that Rumor sends,
By flood and flame, to earth's remotest ends;
War, famine, wreck, and all the varying fates
Of rising cottons, or of falling states;
Revolts at home, and troubles o'er the seas,
Among the Chartists, Affghans, and Chinese;
In all the recent millions that have gone
To the dark realm, and still are hastening on,
That one small tradesman should have joined the throng
Seems a mean theme to babble of in song.
Yet, such is Fame! and such the power of books,
To make small names as deathless as the Duke's:
Yes, the same volume that recordeth you,
Ye mighty chiefs! embalms the printer's too;

And wheresoe'er the poet's fame hath flown,
There, too, the poet's publisher is known;
So shall our friend enjoy, to endless ages,
An immortality — of title-pages.

Methinks I see the Scotsman's canny ghost
Near his old threshold, at his ancient post;
Watching with eager, melancholy face,
The pensive customers that throng the place;
With anxious eye selecting from the throng
Each who has dabbled in this trick of song,
And offering, as of yore, for something nice
In way of epitaph, the market price.
And now his bones the sculptured slab lie under,
What generous bard will *give* him one, I wonder?
For all the golden promises he made;
For all the golden guineas that he paid;
For all the fame his counter could afford
The reverend pamphleteer and author-lord;
For all the pleasant stories he retailed;
And all the turtle, when the stories failed;
For all the praises, all the punch he spent,
What grateful hand will deck his monument?

Campbell 's too proud the compliment to grant;
Southey — for grave and weighty reasons — can't:
Should Moore attempt it, he 'd be sure to cram
John's many virtues in an epigram:
Rogers' blank verse so very blank has grown,
'T would scarce be legible on Parian stone:
Wordsworth would mar it by inscribing on it
A little sermon — what he calls a sonnet.

* Dead.

Alas! for all the guineas that he paid,
And all the immortalities he made,
For all his venison, all his right old wine,
Will none contribute one elegiac line?

In truth, I 'm sad, although I seem to laugh,
To think that John should need an epitaph.
The greatest blows bring not the truest tear,
These minor losses touch the heart more near;
As fewer drops gush over from the eyes
When heroes fall than when your valet dies;
They, of another, an immortal race,
Ne'er seemed on earth well suited with their place,
And, though they yield their transitory breath,
We know their being but begins with death:
When common men — when one like Murray, thus
Is plucked by Death — 't is taking one of us;
And more in his we feel our own decay
Than if a WELLINGTON were snatched away.
'T is not lost genius we lament the most,
No; but the man, the old companion lost:
Who 'd not give more to bring back GILBERT GURNEY,
Or SMITH, or MATTHEWS, from his nether journey,
Than all your MILTONS or your BACONS dead,
Or all the BONAPARTES that ever bled?
So, were the blue rotundity of heaven
By some muck-running, outlawed comet riven,
Should any orb — say yonder blazing Mars —
Be blotted from the muster-roll of stars,
HERSCHEL might groan, or Royal Airy* sigh,
But what would London care? — or you, or I?

* Doctor Airy, Astronomer Royal.

We vulgar folk might count it greater loss,
Should some stray earthquake swallow Charing Cross.

Now let no pigmy poet, in his pride,
The humble memory of our friend deride:
More than he dreams, his little species owe
Those good allies, the Patrons of the Row:
They, only they, of all the friends who praise,
All who forgive, and all who love your lays,
Of all that flatter, all that wish you well,
Sincerely care to have your volume sell.
How oft, when Quarterlies are most severe,
And every critic aims a ready sneer,
And young Ambition just begins to cool,
And Genius half suspects himself a fool,
The placid publisher, the more they rail,
Forebodes the triumph of a speedy sale,
And gently lays the soul-sustaining balm
Of twenty sovereigns in your trembling palm:
While more than speech his manner seems to say,
As bland he whispers, "Dine with me to-day."

Or, when some doubtful bantling of your brain,
Conceived in pleasure, but achieved with pain, —
A bit of satire, or a play, perchance,
A fresh, warm epic, or new-laid romance, —
Receives from all to whom your work you show
Civil endurance, or a faint "so, so;"
When men of taste — men always made of ice —
Cool your gay fancies with a friend's advice;
And prudent fathers, as you read, conceal
With frequent yawn the anger that they feel,

And counsel you to cling to Coke and Chitty,
And leave sweet girls to frame the tuneful ditty,
How oft your MURRAY, with a finer eye,
Detects the gems that mid your rubbish lie;
Instructs you where to alter, where to blot,
And how to trim and patch your faulty plot;
Then bravely buys, and gives you to the town,
The world — the Edinburgh — and your renown!

And, O! how oft, when some dyspeptic swain
Pours forth his agonies in sickly strain,
Mistaking, in the pangs that through him dart,
A wretched liver for a breaking heart;
And prates of passions that he never felt,
And sweats away in vain attempts to melt;
Or takes to brandy, and converts his verse
From sad to savage, nay, begins to curse,
And raves of Nemesis, and hate, and hell,
And smothered woes that in his bosom swell;
When "Newstead" is the name his fancy gives
The snug dominion where he cheaply lives,
And, aping still the aristocratic bard,
With "Crede Jenkins" graved upon his card,
When with his trash he hurries to the press,
Crying "O, print me! print me!" in distress,
Some bookseller, perhaps, most kindly cruel,
Uses the dainty manuscript for fuel!

But all is ended now! John's work is o'er:
He feasts, and pays, and publishes, no more.
Henceforth no volume, save the Book of fate,
Shall bear for him an interest small or great:

And if, in heaven, his literary soul
Walk the pure pavement where the planets roll,
Few old acquaintances will greet him there,
Amid the radiant light and balmy air;
Since few of all who wrote or sang for him
Shall join the anthem of the seraphim.
Yet there might Fancy, in a mood profane,
Behold him listening each celestial strain,
Catching the cadences that sweetly fall,
Wondering if such would sell, below, at all,
And calculating, as they say on earth,
How much those heavenly hymns would there be worth.

Or, if in Proserpine's more sultry zone
For his misdeeds the Publisher must moan,
Though much good company about him stand,
And many an author take him by the hand,
And swarms of novelists around him press,
And many a bard return his warm caress;
Though there on all the sinners he shall gaze
Who ever wrote, or planned, or acted plays;
On all the wits, from Anna's time to ours,
Who strewed perdition's pleasant way with flowers;
On BURNS, consumed with more substantial fire
Than ever love or whiskey could inspire;
On SHELLEY, bathing in a lake of lead,
And BYRON, stretched upon a lava bed;
Little shall he, or they, or any there,
For magazines or morning journals care;
Little shall there be whispered, or be thought,
About the last new book, and what it brought;
Little of copyright and Yankee thieves,
Or any wrong that Dickens' bosom grieves;

But, side by side, reviewer and reviewed,
Critic and criticized, must all be — stewed;
Alas! they groan — alas! compared with this,
Even Blackwood's drunken surgery was bliss.
How less than little were the direst blows
Dealt by brute Gifford on his baby foes!
How light, compared with hell's eternal pain,
The small damnation was of Drury Lane!

Down! down! thou impious, dark Imagination,
Forbear the foul, the blasphemous creation!
Whate'er John's doom, in whatsoever sphere,
Wretched or blest, 't is not for us to hear.
Not many such have dignified his trade,
So boldly bargained and so nobly paid.
O, may his own Divine Paymaster prove
A Judge all mercy in the realms above!

EPISTLE TO WALTER SAVAGE LANDOR.

ON the rough Bracco's top, at break of day,
  High o'er that gulf which bounds the Genoese,
Since thou and I pursued our mountain way,
  Twenty Decembers have disrobed the trees.

So many summers, in their gay return,
  Have found my pilgrimage still incomplete,
Doomed as I seem, Ulysses-like, to earn
  My little knowledge by much toil of feet.

Charmed by the glowing earth and golden sky,
  In Arno's vale you made yourself a nest;
There perched in peace and bookish ease, while I
  Still wandered on — and here am in the West.

And here, amid remembrances that throng
  Thicker than blossoms in the new-born June,
Thine chiefly claims the token of a song
  That still, at least, my heart remains in tune.

But never hope (with so refined a sense
  Of what is well conceived and ably wrought)
To find my verse retain its old pretence
  To the smooth utterance of a pleasing thought.

For who can sing amid this roar of streets,
   This crash of engines and discordant mills?
Where even in Solitude's most lone retreats
   Some factory drowns the music of the rills!

True, Nature here hath donned her gala robe,
   Drest in all charms — soft, savage and sublime;
Within one realm enfolding half the globe,
   Flowers of all soils, and fruits of every clime.

But yet no bard, with consecrating touch,
   Hath made the scene a nobler mood inspire;
The sullen Puritan, the sensual Dutch,
   Proved but a barren fosterage for the lyre!

Imagine old Œnotria as she stood
   In Saturn's reign, before the stranger came;
Ere yet the stillness of the trackless wood
   Had heard the echoes of a Trojan's name.

Young Latium then, as now Missouri's waste,
   Was dumb in story, soulless and unsung:
Whatever deeds her savage annals graced
   Died soon, for want of some harmonious tongue.

Up her dark streams the first explorers found
   Only one dim, interminable shade;
Cliffs with the growth of awful ages crowned,
   Amid whose gloom the wolf and wild-boar preyed.

Afar, perchance, on some cloud-piercing height,
   Nigh the last limit of the eagle's road,
Some stray Pelasgians had assumed a site
   To fix their proud, impregnable abode.

Pent in their airy dens, the builders reared
  Turrets — fanes — altars, fed with daily flame —
But with their walls their memory disappeared:
  Their meanest implements outlive their name!

What race of giants piled yon rocks so high?
  Who cut those hidden channels for the rills?
Drained the deep lake, and sucked the marshes dry,
  Or hollowed into sepulchres the hills?

These, in the time of Romulus, were old;
  Even then, as now, conjecture could but err;
In prose or verse no chronicler hath told
  Whence the tribes came, and who their heroes were.

Their tombs, their sculptures and their funeral urns,
  Which still are mocked by unimproving Art,
Perplex the mind — till tired reflection turns
  To the great people dearer to the heart.

Soon as they rose — the Capitolian lords —
  The land grew sacred and beloved of God;
Where'er they carried their triumphant swords
  Glory sprang forth and sanctified the sod.

Nay, whether wandering by Provincial Rhone,
  Or British Tyne, we note the Cæsar's tracks,
Wondering how far, from their Tarpeian flown,
  The ambitious eagles bore the prætor's axe,

Those toga'd Fathers, those equestrian kings,
  Are still our masters — still within us reign,
Born though we may have been beyond the springs
  Of Britain's floods — beyond the outer main.

For, while the music of their language lasts,
  They shall not perish like the painted men —
Brief-lived in memory as the winter's blasts! —
  Who here once held the mountain and the glen.

From them and theirs with cold regard we turn,
  The wreck of polished nations to survey,
Nor care the savage attributes to learn
  Of souls that struggled with barbarian clay.

With what emotion on a coin we trace
  Vespasian's brow, or Trajan's chastened smile,
But view with heedless eye the murderous mace
  And checkered lance of Zealand's warrior-isle.

Here, by the ploughman, as with daily tread
  He tracks the furrows of his fertile ground,
Dark locks of hair, and thigh-bones of the dead,
  Spear-heads, and skulls, and arrows, oft are found.

On such memorials unconcerned we gaze;
  No trace returning of the glow divine,
Wherewith, dear Walter! in our Eton days
  We eyed a fragment from the Palatine.

It fired us then to trace upon the map
  The forum's line—proud empire's church-yard paths —
Ay, or to finger but a marble scrap
  Or stucco piece from Diocletian's baths.

Cellini's workmanship could nothing add,
  Nor any casket, rich with gems and gold,
To the strange value every pebble had
  O'er which perhaps the Tiber's wave had rolled.

A like enchantment all thy land pervades,
 Mellows the sunshine — softens autumn's breeze —
O'erhangs the mouldering town, and chestnut shades,
 And glows and sparkles in her storied seas.

No such a spell the charmed adventurer guides
 Who seeks those ruins hid in Yucatan,
Where through the tropic forest, silent, glides,
 By crumbled fane and idol, slow Copàn.

There, as the weedy pyramid he climbs,
 Or views, mid groves that rankly wave above,
The work of nameless hands in unknown times,
 Much wakes his wonder — nothing stirs his love.

Art's rude beginnings, wheresoever found,
 The same dull chord of feeling faintly strike;
The Druid's pillar, and the Indian mound,
 And Uxmal's monuments, are mute alike.

Nor here, although the gorgeous year hath brought
 Crimson October's beautiful decay,
Can all this loveliness inspire a thought
 Beyond the marvels of the fleeting day.

For here the Present overpowers the Past;
 No recollections to these woods belong
(O'er which no minstrelsy its veil hath cast),
 To rouse our worship, or supply my song.

But this will come; the necromancer Age
 Shall round the wilderness his glory throw;
Hudson shall murmur through the poet's page,
 And in his numbers more superbly flow.

Enough — 't is more than midnight by the clock;
  Manhattan dreams of dollars, all abed:
With you, dear Walter, 't is the crow of cock,
  And o'er Fièsole the skies are red.

Good-night! yet stay — both longitudes to suit,
  Your own returning, and my absent light,
Thus let me bid our mutual salute;
  To you *buon giorno* — to myself good-night!

MISCELLANEOUS.

ON A BUST OF DANTE.

See, from this counterfeit of him
Whom Arno shall remember long,
How stern of lineament, how grim,
The father was of Tuscan song.
There but the burning sense of wrong,
Perpetual care and scorn, abide;
Small friendship for the lordly throng;
Distrust of all the world beside.

Faithful if this wan image be,
No dream his life was — but a fight;
Could any Beatrice see
A lover in that anchorite?
To that cold Ghibeline's gloomy sight
Who could have guessed the visions came
Of Beauty, veiled with heavenly light,
In circles of eternal flame?

The lips as Cumæ's cavern close,
The cheeks with fast and sorrow thin,
The rigid front, almost morose,
But for the patient hope within,
Declare a life whose course hath been
Unsullied still, though still severe,

Which, through the wavering days of sin,
Kept itself icy-chaste and clear.

Not wholly such his haggard look
When wandering once, forlorn, he strayed,
With no companion save his book,
To Corvo's hushed monastic shade;
Where, as the Benedictine laid
His palm upon the pilgrim guest,
The single boon for which he prayed
The convent's charity was rest.*

Peace dwells not here — this rugged face
Betrays no spirit of repose;
The sullen warrior sole we trace,
The marble man of many woes.
Such was his mien when first arose
The thought of that strange tale divine,
When hell he peopled with his foes,
The scourge of many a guilty line.

War to the last he waged with all
The tyrant canker-worms of earth;
Baron and duke, in hold and hall,
Cursed the dark hour that gave him birth;
He used Rome's harlot for his mirth;
Plucked bare hypocrisy and crime;
But valiant souls of knightly worth
Transmitted to the rolls of Time.

* It is told of DANTE that, when he was roaming over Italy, he came to a certain monastery, where he was met by one of the friars, who blessed him, and asked what was his desire; to which the weary stranger simply answered, "*Pace.*"

O, Time! whose verdicts mock our own,
The only righteous judge art thou;
That poor, old exile, sad and lone,
Is Latium's other VIRGIL now:
Before his name the nations bow;
His words are parcel of mankind,
Deep in whose hearts, as on his brow,
The marks have sunk of DANTE's mind.

PARAPHRASE OF A PASSAGE IN DANTE:

PARADISO, CANTO XXI.

The poet meets in Paradise the spirit of San Pietro Damiano, a man famous, in his time, for the purity and austerity of his life, and for his endeavors to reform the dissolute habits of the Romish clergy in that age, and the pompous luxury of their prelates.

It is supposed that he was born in Ravenna, about 1007. Having withdrawn from the world into the monastery of Santa Croce di Fonte Avellana, he was called from this retirement and employed in many important missions, in which he showed so much ability that he was made Cardinal and Bishop of Ostia. Landino says that he was not merely called, but forcibly compelled to this dignity.

The subjoined paraphrase has so little claim to any exactness, that the thirty lines of the original have been amplified into ninety. It is hoped there may be found a closer adherence to the *spirit* of the text — and of San Damiano. That the scholar may judge for himself, the whole passage is appended.

Between the Hadrian and the Tyrrhene shores,
  And not far distant from the Tuscan line,
A jutting crag above the thunder soars,
  Cresting with ridgy rocks the Apennine.
Catria 't is called, and oft the tempest roars
  Down in the region of the fig and vine,

Tra due liti d' Italia surgon sassi,
E non molto distanti alla tua patria,
Tanto, che i tuoni assai suonan più bassi;
  E fanno un gibbo, che si chiama Catria,
Disotto al quale è consecrato un ermo,

While sunny Catria shines in cloudless June;
  And at its foot a consecrated cell
From the rough granite opens, rudely-hewn,
  A fit abode for one who bids farewell
To life's harsh jar, desiring to attune
  His thoughts to heaven, and in seclusion dwell.

There, in my peaceful hermitage, serene,
  I with so constant zeal my God obeyed,
That, with continual fasts and vigils lean,
  Through summer heats and winter frosts I prayed.
Clad in a garment like my Saviour's, mean,
  Of simple olives my repast I made;

And, on the great hereafter wholly bent,
  Weeding the garden of my soul from sin,
The lonely meditative hours I spent,
  Above the busy world's distracting din.
And joyous, in my rocky cloister pent,
  Abundant harvests did I gather in,

Upon that bleak and barren cliff, to pour
  Into the garners of the Lord — alas!
That sacred seat is hallowed now no more
  By morning orisons or midnight mass,
Or sandalled anchorite that numbers o'er
  His holy beads as the slow moments pass.

Che suol esser disposto a sola làtria.
  Così ricominciommi il terzo sermo;
E poi continuando disse: quivi
Al servigio di Dio mi fei sì fermo
  Che pur con cibi di liquor d' ulivi
Lievemente passava e caldi e gieli,
Contento ne' pensier contemplativi

But now, sole occupant, the lizard crawls
At noon-day round my desolate retreat;
Nor ever sanctified are those rude walls
By the blest echoes of a pilgrim's feet;
And with a low, reproachful murmur falls
The rill beside my old accustomed seat,

Where, day by day, at Avellana's fount,
By men Pietro Damiano named,
Strict in my stewardship's exact account,
And through Romagna for my penance famed,
I sat and mused on mine adopted mount,
Serving my Master with a life unblamed.

Ah! what availed it that an abbey rose
With pillared pomp my modest rock to grace;
In those cold aisles Devotion's essence froze,
Dearer to Heaven was that sequestered place
Which for my chapel and my cave I chose,
Wherein, recluse, to run my godly race.

But Honors came — and Pomp found out my nest,
And like a weak hare I was hunted down;
They planted vanities within my breast,

Render solea quel chiostro a questi cieli
Fertilemente, ed ora è fatto vano,
Sì che tosto convien che si riveli.
In quel loco fu' io Pier Damiano;
E Pietro Peccator fu nella casa
Di Nostra Donna in sul lito Adriano.
Poca vita mortal m' era rimasa,
Quando fui chiesto e tratto a quel cappello,
Che pur di male in peggio si travasa.

And robed my shoulders with the scarlet gown.
Then my long days of pensiveness and rest
Were poorly bartered for the world's renown.

To Rome they dragged me, and my thin white hairs
Were by the Cardinal's red hat concealed;
There the harsh lessons of my daily cares
Disclosed new truths and hidden wrongs revealed.
For soon I learned how oft the priesthood wears
Its reverend garb for Vice a mask and shield;

I saw the pride, the falsehood of their state;
I saw the low, the sensual and the vain,
Implored for pardon and dispensing fate;
I saw them fawn and flatter, trick and feign;
I saw their outward smiles and hidden hate,
Their lust and luxury, and thirst for gain.

Saint Peter barefoot on his mission came,
And Paul, a "chosen vase," in whom was poured
So lavishly the heavenly spirit's flame,
Snatched his chance meal at any casual board;
And, reckoning honest poverty no shame,
Above all wants in lofty virtue soared.

Venne Cephas, e venne il gran vasello
Dello Spirito Santo, magri e scalzi,
Prendendo il cibo di qualunque ostello.
Or voglion quinci e quindi chi rincalzi
Gli moderni pastori, e chi gli meni,
Tanto son gravi, e chi dirietro gli alzi.
Cuopron de' manti loro i palafreni,
Sì che due bestie van sott' una pelle:
O pazienza, che tanto sostieni!

Oft in the Lateran I thought of this,
  Amid the tinselled priests' tumultuous tread,
As on the congregations, bowed submiss,
  Its fragrant shower the fuming censer shed;
And some stooped low the foot of him to kiss
  Whose master "had not where to lay his head."

And when I 've seen, on some high holiday,
  Through the live streets their long processions roll,
And the fat, ermined friars, on palfreys gay, —
  Both creatures covered with one furry stole, — *
Him I remembered, robed in mean array,
  Who entered Zion on an ass's foal.

He like an humble peasant meekly rode,
  While shouted forth Jerusalem a song,
And with palm-boughs his gladsome pathway strewed;
  Our modern pastors need a hand full strong
On either side to prop their helpless load;
  O, patience! patience! that endur'st so long!

* "Both *beasts* furred over with a single stole," or, "two beasts under one skin," would be nearer to Dante's expression; but the worthy Jesuit, the Padre Venturi, cries out upon this — "*motto plebeo, e da mercato vecchio!*"

A PAGE OF CONCHOLOGY.

What god it was I cannot say,
   But one there was, when Jove was king,
Who, wandering by some Grecian bay,
   Picked up a vacant shell that lay
Bleached on the shore, a dry, unsavory thing.

Nor is my memory well informed
   (No Lemprière 's at hand to blab)
What tenant had this mansion warmed;
   Something with which the Ægean swarmed,
Some lobster, I suppose it was, or crab.

But he, the cunning brat of heaven,
   Trimmed it according to his wish,
Crossed it with fibres, — three, or seven,
   Or, as Pausanias thinks, eleven,—
And gave a language to the poor, dead fish.

At once, the house, which, e'en when filled
   By its old habitant, was dumb,
Now, as the immortal artist willed,
   A little sea-Odèon trilled,
And trembled low to the celestial thumb.

Enraptured with his new invention,
  Up soared he to the blissful seat,
And, having caught even Jove's attention,
  And calmed a family dissension,
Went serenading through the starry street.

With us, the story 's the reverse :
  Our souls are born already strung,
But, 'twixt the cradle and the hearse,
  Creeps a change o'er us — for the worse!
The heart hath music only when 't is young.

For soon there comes a sordid god,
  Who snaps the precious chords of sound,
And leaves the soul an empty pod,
  A yellow husk, — a dull, hard clod, —
A faded shell, in which no voice is found.

Save when some bold, heroic hand,
  That dares to strike the tyrant, Time,
Tries its first impulse to command,
  And, thrilling through the startled land,
Wastes the last ebbings of his youth in rhyme.

THE INTELLECTUAL REPUBLIC:

WRITTEN FOR THE BOSTON LYCEUM, NOVEMBER 19, 1840.

Already graced with Bravery's martial crown,
Our young republic pants for fresh renown;
When idle Prowess finds no scene for fame,
Some loftier glory beams, in Virtue's name;
Reposing Valor wantons in a trance
Of calm Philosophy, or gay Romance;
Refinement blooms, and Wisdom claims the wreath
Which silver hairs, not scars, are hid beneath.
In every state, as one heroic age,
One intellectual, stands on history's page.
Now maddening nations quit their tranquil farms
To swell the fight — a universe in arms!
Now Strife, his work beginning to abhor,
Bids tired Augustus close the gates of War;
Hushed is the trump — a milder sway succeeds,
Now peaceful Georgics wake the Mantuan reeds.
Such days beheld the Stoic porch arise,
With Academia — garden of the wise!
Then Epicurus taught his gentle train
The dulcet musings of a doubtful brain,
And Plato — bee-lipped oracle! — beguiled
His loved Lyceum, listening like a child.

Thus eras change, and such a change is ours;
Rough Mars gives way to April's promised flowers:
Forth springs the god-like intellect, unchained;
Guard it, good angels! keep it unprofaned;
Guide it, lest, lured by offices or gold,
Its rights be bartered, and its empire sold.
Now books accomplish what the sword began,
Wide spreads the rule of educated man,
No let, no limit, to its march sublime,
In space, but ocean — in duration, Time.
So swift its course, some prophet may contend
Its very progress bodes a speedy end:
No! like Niagara's changeless current driven,
It moves, yet stays, eternal as the heaven:
That mighty torrent, as it flows to-day,
Forever flows, but never flows away;
The waves you gazed at yesterday are gone,
Yet the same restless deluge thunders on.
As crumble Custom's mouldering chains with rust,
Power's gilded idol tumbles to the dust.
Tradition totters from her cloudy throne,
And all the impostures of the past are known.
Hardly can *we* lend credence to the tale
Of their long woes who first rent error's veil:
What royal spite, what curses from the Church,
Awed the pale scholar in his cloistered search;
How many from themselves their visions hid,
Or wandered exiles, outcast and forbid,
Like Dante, scaling with dejected tread
A tyrant's stairs, to taste his bitter bread!
Think how Columbus toiled, through years of pain,
For leave to try the secret of the main;

Yet the dream dawned, and gave, in spite of Rome,
Spain a new world, and half mankind a home.

Unhappy days! when they who read the stars
Oft only saw them through their dungeon bars:
Our tutored minds less dangerous ways explore, —
The immortal pioneers have gone before.
As the worn bark, no more to storms a sport,
Just makes the headland of her opening port,
New perils then awake the master's dread,
Anxious he walks, and eyes the frequent lead;
But, if the pilot come, he yields the helm,
And stands a subject in his floating realm,
The veteran's nod his mariners obey,
And wind confiding on their shoaly way.
Like them we travel, safely gliding by
Opinion's thousand wrecks that round us lie.
Not thus were you, ye leader spirits! taught
Your pathway, beaconed through the wilds of thought:
For you no Newton yet had poised the world,
No sage La Place heaven's glittering leaves unfurled,
But each suspicion of the truth was born
A dim conjecture, heralding the morn.
Thus from his height bewildered Kepler strayed,
To toy with vain Chaldea's mystic trade,
And sought in yon blue labyrinth to behold
Man's life and fortunes lustrously foretold.
Hence Danish Tycho's heavenly city swarmed
With crude ideas, and fantasies deformed.
Yet, sparely blame! nor be extreme to mark
Their faulty light, when all was else — how dark!

But now the Mind, from ancient falsehood woke,
Abjures old Superstition's rotten yoke:
No wrathful threat in Nature's thunder fears,
No fate predicted by the falling spheres.
All childish fables, Fancy's fond pretence,
Fade from the cold arithmetic of Sense:
No jocund Fauns through copse or prairie rove,
No dripping Naiads haunt the godless grove;
And had no holier new Religion given
More certain tokens of a purer heaven,
By fount, and rock, and by the sounding shore,
Nothing were left to dream of and adore.
Now to Truth's courts, a never-faltering throng,
Thy torch, O Science! lights and leads along.
No sluggard sons this age of labor owns,
In earth's great workshop solitary drones,
But every mind the general task must share,
Brave the long toil and mingle in the care,
In love with Knowledge, that alone can be
Our country's hope — sole safeguard of the free.

AUGUST, 1840.

THE PEOPLE OF THE DEEP.

Never hath navigator found
   A nook where mortals have not been;
The floods are full — all seas abound
   With myriads of our kin;
And more humanity lies hidden
   Fathomless leagues below the surge,
Than o'er its surface, tempest-ridden,
   Their peopled navies urge.

Becalmed at midnight, on the deep,
   Soon as our second watch was set,
On the damp deck I dropped asleep,
   All troubles to forget.
But in my brain, that would not slumber,
   Loved forms and lovely faces thronged,
Friends past my power to name or number,
   And some to heaven belonged.

But one sweet shape, of beauty strange,
   Broke my bright vision with a kiss;
I started — ah! the bitter change,
   From blessed dreams to this!
For, ah! how silent, dark, and lonely,
   These melancholy deserts are;
No life, save yon tired helmsman only,
   Nor light, — save here and there a star.

The drowsy mariner's dull tread
  Is the sole sound that wakes mine ears;
How hushed! how desolate and dead
  Creation's void appears!
"Thou dumb, thou lonely, lonely ocean!"
  Chilled by my fancies, I began, —
"Fearful in stillness as in motion,
  Thou art no place for man!

"Earth's wildernesses, everywhere,
  Teem with some records of our race;
Even waste Palenque's fragments bear
  Life's annals on their face.
But you, ye solitary waters!
  What memories can ye recall?
Better to speak of crime and slaughters
  Than tell no tale at all.

"Hark! to that heavy-breathing sound,
  That seems the moaning of the sea;
Or, of some whale, on whose own ground
  Rude trespassers are we.
This is Leviathan's dominion,
  Where man is rash to stray —
Ah, might I borrow but thy pinion,
  Swift sea-gull! for a day,

"This element, for monsters made,
  Full swiftly would I leave behind,
And friends amid the forest shade
  In gentler creatures find."

Thus musing, sleep again stole o'er me,
   And voices, in my second dream,
Came from a throng which rose before me —
   "How falsely dost thou deem!

"Behold! thy brethren fill the waves,
   All the great gulfs are amply stored."
And, lo! from forth their coral caves
   The ocean dwellers poured.
"We are the people of the waters!"
   Faintly they gurgled in mine ear;
"Fathers and mothers — sons and daughters —
   Old age and youth are here."

The scaly multitudes that swarm
   In the green shelter of the bay,
Chased by the fury of the storm,
   Less numerous were than they.
They came in armies, thickly crowding,
   Fleshless and dripping, bleached and bare;
Sea-plants their bony bosoms shrouding,
   Sands glistening in their hair.

"See! see!" they cried, "what legions strew
   The sparkling pavement of the brine!
Our ancient universe below
   Is populous as thine.
But wheresoe'er war's banners flying
   Have brought the fleets of England's host,
There, foe by foe, together lying,
   Our nations cluster most.

" Many and large our cities are,
Wide scattered over ocean's floor;
Some of us dwell near Trafalgar,
And some at Elsinore.
Some that were enemies, now brothers,
Linger about the immortal isle
Of Grecian Salamis, — and others
Rest in the freshness of the Nile."

" Home! home! poor spectres," I replied,
" Till the seas dry at trump of doom;
Earth and her waters — far and wide —
Are only one huge tomb.
Till now I thought the main's chief treasure
Was pearls and heaps of jewels rare;
But, ah! what wealth, beyond all measure,
In mine own shape lies there!"

Then, musing on the valor, worth,
And beauty, dwelling in the deep,
And the mean brood that God's good earth
In their possession keep,
I almost wished my parting minute
Might find me somewhere on the wave,
That I might join the brave within it,
And no man dig my grave.

THRENODIA.

ON THE DEATH OF PRESIDENT HARRISON.

Spoken by Mr. Vandenhoff, the elder, at the Tremont Theatre, April 13, 1841.

STUNNED is the nation with a troublous knell!
The pulse of triumph had not all grown calm:
But the shouts are hushed — and the trumpet swell·
For the sudden sound of a passing bell
Hath changed our pæan to a funeral psalm!

Scarce had the note of our rejoicing woke
The wilds of Oregon, — and now a wail
Through the forest comes, and the dulling stroke
Of the muffled drum, and the volleyed smoke
And roar of cannon, blend with April's gale.

Beyond Missouri's farthest-rising springs,
The wandering tribes shall catch the mingled tone,
And be dumb, in listening the tale it brings,
How the father-chief of their prairie kings
To the Great Spirit's council-watch hath gone!

Fell not our chieftain as a soldier ought?
'T was Victory's voice that whispered him to rest;
And of all the garlands his virtues brought,
'T is the *last* shall dwell in his country's thought,
Longer than all his Leuctras* in the West.

* Epaminondas.

In Glory's field full many a laurel grows
  For him, — but conquest yields no equal crown
To the civic wreath which a land bestows
On the veteran head, where the sacred snows,
  Printed with goodness, cover past renown.

Sum then his fortunes by the final day,
  And count him blest; — Napoleon might have given
Marengo's fame, to have passed away
With as peaceful a sigh from his hold of clay,
  With no man's curse to hinder him from heaven.

TO A "MAGDALEN."

A PAINTING BY GUIDO.

I.

Mary, when thou wert a virgin,
  Ere the first, the fatal sin
Stole into thy bosom's chamber,
  Leading six companions in;
Ere those eyes had wept an error,
  What thy beauty must have been!

II.

Ere those lips had paled their crimson,
  Quivering with the soul's despair,
Ere the smile they wore had withered
  In thine agony of prayer,
Or, instead of pearls, the tear-drops
  Gleamed amid thy streaming hair.

III.

While, in ignorance of evil,
  Still thy heart serenely dreamed,
And the morning light of girlhood
  On thy cheeks' young garden beamed,
Where the abundant rose was blushing,
  Not of earth couldst thou have seemed!

IV.

When thy frailty fell upon thee,
  Lovely wert thou, even then;
Shame itself could scarce disarm thee
  Of the charms that vanquished men;
Which of Salem's purest daughters
  Matched the sullied MAGDALEN?

V.

But thy MASTER's eye beheld thee,
  Foul and all unworthy heaven;
Pitied, pardoned, purged thy spirit
  Of its black, pernicious leaven;
Drove the devils from out the temple,
  All the dark, the guilty seven.*

VI.

O, the beauty of repentance!
  MARY, ten-fold fairer now
Art thou with dishevelled tresses,
  And that anguish on thy brow;
Ah, might every sinful sister
  Grow in beauty, ev'n as thou!

* "Mary, from whom were cast *seven* devils."

LIVORNO.

Where Smollet sleeps, in Leghorn, there is buried,
Amid the graves of many English strangers,
One of our countrymen, — a nameless being, —
Whose mound is only marked by one blank slab,
Half-hid in hyacinths, that bloom unbidden
Beneath the tread of every idler's foot.
His home and cradle was the Hampshire hills,
Further than Britain, more remote than Thule,
Where the blue Merrimac's first fountain springs.
There had he wandered, in his early days,
By rock and brook, with Fancy for his playmate,
Full of the world that learning had unlocked.
His brain was peopled with departed heroes, —
Troy's roving emigrants, the Latian sires,
The men of history and the gods of Greece.
The master minds whose mighty phantoms walk
In academic halls, or volumed lie
In close companionship on college shelves,
Where in the dust rich thoughts like jewels hide,
Had warmed him into worship of the past.
His heart was written o'er, like some stray page
Torn out from Plutarch, with majestic names;
People and places of antique renown;

Founders of kingdoms, consuls, orators,
And chiefs who swell the chronicles of Rome.
With these he lived, almost himself a Roman;
Wearing his camlet as it were a toga,
Thinking in Latin, absent in his answers,
Heedless of what was round him, and belonging
Rather to Tully's period than his own.
Where'er he wandered, — whether to the shore,
Or mid the new-built nests of busy Thrift,
Springing as Thebes did at Amphion's playing,
To the dull drone of inharmonious mills, —
Where'er chance led him, he transformed the scene,
Giving Soracte's name to Kearsàrge,
And styling "preceps Anio" that which men
Call Amonòosac in the vulgar diction.
   But Fancy rests not long content with fancies;
If so, no marriages would spring from sonnets;
Ambition, satisfied with smoke, would loll,
Pleased with his pipe, upon a silken sofa;
And all the restless multitude who fly,
Canvas or vapor-winged, beyond the seas,
In quest of ruins, pictures and warm winters,
Would lie abed and gaze on Europe's chart,
Travelling more snugly on their chamber wainscot.
Prudent are they who never stir from home,
Save in conception; who beside their fire
Securely wander, only in a book,
And find adventures in another's rambles.
To such a modest wisher 't were enough
To hear of music, and to smell a feast,
To talk by letter merely, with a sweetheart,
And only worship beauty's marble image.

Such airy diet suited not the taste
Of him I speak of; hungry was his heart
For the reality of all the dreams
Which fed his boyhood; — how he longed to see
Italy's earth! the actual stones of Rome;
To touch the Capitol, and with proud foot
Tread the same pavement Cicero had walked on!
This was his one desire; for this he dimmed
His watchful eyes with midnight occupations,
Thinning his tresses with consuming studies,
And drying up with toil the sap of youth,
Which gathers most, like dew-drops, in the night,
When slumber comes like evening to the roses.
Little by little, had he won the means
Whereby men master fortune; power was his
To make the earth his turnpike, every gate
Readily opening to the magic toll
Which wise men bear like amulets about them,
To charm away that worst disorder — want.
Then came the time of Love, — the common story, —
Fair was the lady; ye, whose road has led you
Amid the western valleys of New England
By Housatonic, you may guess how fair.
She, too, had learned, and partly caught of him,
That adoration of the antique world,
Which many thousand miles of briny distance
Hallow in thought as potently as Time.
Oft would she listen, as they sat by night,
Watching the fireflies, to the brave description
Of those unnumbered lights which, every Easter,
Kindle St. Peter's cupola, while Heaven
Withholds its stars, as fearing to be shamed

By the gay glory of the girandòle!
And oft when walking in the village church-yard,
Among the mounds where humble farmers rested,
He told her of Metella's tomb, and Virgil's,
The Scipios' vault with those which line the Appian,
And that gray pyramid within whose shade
Sleeps the Septemvir with his English guests,
Cestius and Shelley and — O, Friend! thou knowest, —
Or if they looked from Holyoke o'er the meadows,
He took her with him, on the wings of thought,
To green Campania, showed her sunny Naples,
Stretched out like one of her own lazzaroni,
In smiling indolence, along the shore;
Your villas, Baiæ! thy dumb temples, Pæstum!
Where meditation makes the only worship;
Vineyards whose juices, drawn from buried cities,
Taste of the times of Flaccus and Tibullus,
And whirl the memory twenty centuries back.
  Happy! yes, happier than they knew they were,
These lovers thus indulged their dreams together,
More blest for knowing not that this was bliss.
The days we spend unconscious of delight
Are those which most delight us in remembrance,
And the sweet minutes which are spent in hope
Make hope's accomplishment a dull content.
  Two drops that meet and make a single drop
Mingle not more instinctively than souls
Thus brought together, side by side, as 't were,
On the same stem and leaf of our existence.
Scarce were their bridal holidays well o'er,
When the great Wish which many years had nourished,
The golden frame-work of such goodly pictures,

Approached completion. Look! a ship is ready;
Her canvas full-fed with the generous wind,
Whose course is destined for the rocky gate
Of that famed sea whose legendary name,
"Mediterranean," breathes of history.
And they are in that vessel; — farewell, home!
Farewell, America! with all thy names,
Which sound unused and dissonant in song,
Yet no less precious to the heart for that.
We 're for the land whose daily talk is music;
We 're bound for Italy, our port is Naples;
Dulcet Parthenope! Torquato's cradle,
And Maro's resting-place; amid such words,
How hard in verse to say, Farewell, New York!
So sink the hills of Neversink behind them,
And the New World is but a thing to talk of:
And life no longer is a stated task
To be encountered and performed for wages;
But the free kisses of the laughing ocean
Seem to invite the madly-bounding prow
To leap and dance on the deep's foamy floor,
To the glad tunes of the resounding billows.
The mariners, 't would seem, were following simply
Their inclination rather than their calling;
The chains of Drudgery seemed to drop away,
And life's main duty, merely life and motion.
Careless existence! how the occupations,
Troubles and fretful interests of the shore,
With the shore vanish! Earth is only earthly
To the dull souls that burrow on the land.
Such was their ecstasy at first, but soon
The rapture lessened, and with every sun

The strand they sailed from dearer grew and fairer,
And that whereto each billow brought them nearer
Lost the fine surface of the bright romance
Whose brilliancy is born of distance only;
So to the greedy Spaniards in Peru
The rocks of lime on Illiassa's height,
Beheld afar, seemed hills of purest silver;
And the brown husks which roofed the Indian huts
Solid and beaten plates of virgin gold;
Nay, this dim ball, this murky lump, this earth,
Seen from yon Venus, were as bright as she.

THE GROOMSMAN TO HIS MISTRESS.

I.

Every wedding, says the proverb,
  Makes another, soon or late;
Never yet was any marriage
  Entered in the book of Fate,
But the names were also written
  Of the patient pair that wait.

II.

Blessings then upon the morning
  When my friend, with fondest look,
By the solemn rites' permission,
  To himself his mistress took,
And the Destinies recorded
  Other two within their book.

III.

While the priest fulfilled his office,
  Still the ground the lovers eyed,
And the parents and the kinsmen
  Aimed their glances at the bride,
But the groomsmen eyed the virgins
  Who were waiting at her side.

IV.

Three there were that stood beside her;
   One was dark, and one was fair,
But nor fair nor dark the other,
   Save her Arab eyes and hair;
Neither dark nor fair I call her,
   Yet she was the fairest there.

V.

While her groomsman — shall I own it ?
   Yes, to thee, and only thee —
Gazed upon this dark-eyed maiden
   Who was fairest of the three,
Thus he thought : "How blest the bridal
   Where the bride were such as she ! "

VI.

Then I mused upon the adage,
   Till my wisdom was perplexed,
And I wondered, as the churchman
   Dwelt upon his holy text,
Which of all who heard his lesson
   Should require the service next.

VII.

Whose will be the next occasion
   For the flowers, the feast, the wine ?
Thine perchance, my dearest lady,
   Or, who knows ? — it may be mine :
What if 't were — forgive the fancy —
   What if 't were — both mine and thine ?

CAMPANILE DI PISA.

Snow was glistening on the mountains, but the air was that of June,
Leaves were falling, but the runnels playing still their summer tune,
And the dial's lazy shadow hovered nigh the brink of noon.
On the benches in the market rows of languid idlers lay,
When to Pisa's nodding belfry, with a friend, I took my way.

From the top we looked around us, and as far as eye might strain,
Saw no sign of life or motion, in the town, or on the plain;
Hardly seemed the river moving, through the willows to the main;
Nor was any noise disturbing Pisa from her drowsy hour,
Save the doves that fluttered 'neath us, in and out, and round the
tower.

Not a shout from gladsome children, or the clatter of a wheel,
Nor the spinner of the suburb winding his discordant reel,
Nor the stroke upon the pavement of a hoof or of a heel:
Even the slumberers, in the church-yard of the Campo Santo, seemed
Scarce more quiet than the living world that underneath us dreamed.

Dozing at the city's portal, heedless guard the sentry kept,
More than oriental dulness o'er the sunny farms had crept,
Near the walls the ducal herdsman by the dusty road-side slept;

While his camels,* resting round him, half alarmed the sullen ox,
Seeing those Arabian monsters pasturing with Etruria's flocks.

Then it was, like one who wandered, lately, singing by the Rhine,
Strains† perchance to maiden's hearing sweeter than this verse of mine,
That we bade Imagination lift us on her wing divine.
And the days of Pisa's greatness rose from the sepulchral past,
When a thousand conquering galleys bore her standard at the mast.

Memory for a moment crowned her sovereign mistress of the seas,
When she braved, upon the billows, Venice and the Genoese,
Daring to deride the Pontiff, though he shook his angry keys.
When her admirals triumphant, riding o'er the Soldan's waves,
Brought from Calvary's holy mountain fitting soil for knightly graves.

When the Saracen surrendered, one by one, his pirate isles,
And Ionia's marble trophies decked Lungarno's Gothic piles,
Where the festal music floated in the light of ladies' smiles;
Soldiers in the busy court-yard, nobles in the halls above —
O! those days of arms are over — arms and courtesy and love!

Down in yonder square at sunrise, lo! the Tuscan troops arrayed,
Every man in Milan armor, forged in Brescia every blade:
Sigismondi is their captain — Florence! art thou not dismayed?

* Near Pisa, a herd of camels is kept, upon a farm belonging to the Grand Duke. The ancestors of these animals were brought thither during the crusades. Some of them are employed in the work of the farm, and others may be met straying about in the pine woods or along the sands of the coast.

"These sands, with the sea, the camels, the purity and brightness of the sky, the solitude and silence, give this picture something oriental, novel and poetical, which pleases the fancy, and transports it to the desert." — VALERY.

† The Belfry of Bruges.

There 's Lanfranchi! there the bravest of the Gherardesca stem,
Hugolino — with the bishop — but enough — enough of them.

Now, as on Achilles' buckler, next a peaceful scene succeeds;
Pious crowds in the cathedral duly tell their blessed beads;
Students walk the learned cloister — Ariosto wakes the reeds —
Science dawns — and Galileo teaches now the Italian youth,
As he were a new Columbus, new discovered realms of truth.

Hark! what murmurs from the million in the bustling market rise!
All the lanes are loud with voices, all the windows dark with eyes;
Black with men the marble bridges, heaped the shores with merchandise;
Turks and Greeks and Libyan merchants in the square their councils hold,
And the Christian altars glitter, gorgeous with Byzantine gold!

Look! anon the masqueraders don their holiday attire;
Every palace is illumined — all the town seems built of fire —
Rainbow-colored lanterns dangle from the top of every spire:
Pisa's patron saint hath hallowed to himself the joyful day,
Never on the thronged Rialto showed the Carnival more gay.

Suddenly the bell beneath us broke the vision with its chime;
"Signors," quoth our gray attendant, "it is almost vesper time;"
Vulgar life resumed its empire — down we dropt from the sublime.
Here and there a friar passed us, as we paced the silent streets,
And a cardinal's rumbling carriage roused the sleepers from the seats.

SAINT VALENTINE'S DAY.

THIS day was sacred, once, to Pan,
  And kept with song and wine;
But when our better creed began
  'T was held no more divine,
Until there came a holy man,
  One Bishop Valentine.

He, finding, as all good men will,
  Much in the ancient way
That was not altogether ill,
  Restored the genial day,
And we the pagan fashion still
  With pious hearts obey.

Without this custom, all would go
  Amiss in Love's affairs,
All passion would be poor dumb show,
  Pent sighs, and secret prayers;
And bashful maids would never know
  What timid swain was theirs.

Ah! many things with mickle pains
  Without reward are done,
A thousand poets rack their brains
  For her who loves but one;

Yea, many weary with their strains
   The nymph that cares for none.

Yet, should no faithful heart be faint
   To give affection's sign:
So, dearest, let mine own acquaint
   With its emotions — thine;
And blessings on that fine old Saint,
   Good Bishop Valentine!

A SARATOGA ECLOGUE.

MELIBŒUS.

WHILE you, my TITYRUS, beneath the shade
Of Congress Hall's pine-pillared colonnade,
Suck in the sweet oblivion of your smoke,
Ejecting now a puff and now a joke,
Say, will not Fancy, spite of your cigar,
And all the strong nepenthes of the bar,
At times fly back from woods and country air
To busy Broad-street, and the warehouse there?

TITYRUS.

O, MELIBŒUS, think not for myself
I laid my ledger on the guarded shelf,
Locked my big safe, and bade my clerks disperse
To fish for trout, shoot bears, or scribble verse:
Bushes and groves are dismal sights to me;
I love a lamp-post better than a tree,
Save those that grow by gas-light, in the Park,
With play-bill aprons on their decent bark;
Nor know I any verdure like the greens
In Fulton market — curse your sylvan scenes!
Small wish had I to taste this rustic life;
No, MELIBŒUS, 't was to please my wife.

MELIBŒUS.

Then disappointment is your just reward:
I have a wife, but I am sovereign lord;
Right well she knows, the woman being wise,
In me alone the choice of journey lies;
Lamb-like she follows, to the Springs or Falls —
Where'er my whim or my dyspepsia calls.
Ass that I was! about the end of June
I found my bowels getting out of tune;
Naught but these waters, my physician said,
Could quell the bile, or calm the throbbing head:
Quick to anticipate the coming swarm
That take the country every year by storm, —
Rushing like haggard shadows to the Styx,
Or greedy bisons to the briny licks, —
Hither I sped, and, raptured with the spot,
Hired half an acre, with a cow and cot.
Mine was the blunder, mine is the regret;
And mine, beside, the same dyspepsia yet;
And more it vexes me that here I came,
Having no wife, like you, to share the blame.

TITYRUS.

I blame not mine; I only told you why
I fled from town; a gentler husband I.
I let my love in minor matters rule;
She where she pleaseth sends the girls to school:
She orders dinner; she decides what sect
Shall number us among its pure elect;
Whate'er her taste, secure of suiting me,
Venison or duck, one deity or three.

When dog-days came, she fancied these famed waters
Would benefit her spirits and my daughters;
Thrice every day the sluggish pool they drink,
Six tingling tumblers, down without a wink!
But I confess that simple Croton's flood,
Though it give no magnesia to the blood,
More suits my liking ——

MELIBŒUS.

Ay, with something in 't, —
A scrap of lemon, or a sprig of mint.

TITYRUS.

And as for air, what air can equal ours?
Do you admire the sweetness of the flowers?

MELIBŒUS.

Not I: these breezes are but pap to me;
I love the ham-like relish of the sea.

TITYRUS

Our nostrils here how little flavor greets,
Compared with all the spiciness of streets!
The thousand odors from ambrosial shops,
To catch whose balm the rustic stranger stops;
Barrows of pine-apples, and trays of tarts,
The breath of new-born loaves from baker's carts;
The steams oft gushing, as your head you droop,
Up from some subterranean realm of soup.

MELIBŒUS.

The pleasant whiffs of terrapin, — the smell
Of oyster-shops, — I also know them well;

Well you recall them to my mental nose;
Ah! could art graft such odors on a rose!
Or, O! that any flower, tree, shrub, or grass,
Might imitate the perfume of the gas!

TITYRUS.

O, balmy gas! that might almost persuade
A wood-born Dryad to forswear the shade,
How much of happiness its name recalls!
Club-rooms, and reading-rooms, and social halls;
Concerts and theatres, and midnight cells,
Where blushing lobsters doff their bashful shells,
And Liebfraumilch — right worthy of its name! —
Glides, like the milk of kindness, through your frame.

MELIBŒUS.

In my young days, ere steam with magic leap
Had, by abridging, almost bridged the deep,
I crossed the seas, and, wandering Europe through,
With each great city so familiar grew,
That, were I blindfold travelling, I could tell
My whereabout correctly, by the smell.
From that long pilgrimage returning home,
Ere steeple hove in sight, or tower or dome,
Far o'er the bitter desert of the brine
I knew my birth-place by the smell of swine
For dear Manhattan was a village then,
And its pig population matched its men.

TITYRUS.

Once to New Bedford in a smack I sailed,
When one dense fog both land and ocean veiled,

Yet little seemed the master to perplex —
A tough, dry man, whom vapors could not vex.
"Captain, your course is guess-work now," said I;
"I *nose* my reckoning," was his queer reply;
No beacon guided him, nor buoy, nor star,
But the train-oil he scented from afar.

MELIBŒUS.

In oriental climes, but not far down,
Lies Marblehead — ancient and fish-like town;
Rich less in pastures than in sunburnt rocks,
Her salted cod are all her herds and flocks;
Beside her cod, a hardy race she breeds,
Whom the storms cradle and the ocean feeds:
When one of these bold mariners, her boast,
Returns from Ind, or California's coast,
Soon as the gulf-stream he hath left behind,
If haply come a puff of western wind,
Long ere the cow can scent the distant sod,
He snuffs afar his country and his cod:
Hangs o'er the rail, and, half a woman grown,
Adds to the brine some droppings of his own:
Home swells his heart — the throne of every wish —
O home! O friends! O fireside! and O fish!

TITYRUS.

Strong in some natures is the nasal sense —
To them each odor hath its eloquence;
With some, Remembrance holds her secret reign
In the proboscis, rather than the brain;
While in more stolid ones, of ruder make,
Scarcely could onions an emotion wake.

But tell me now, so gifted as thou art
With nicer nerves, that speak a warmer heart,
Tell, if thy memory match thy smelling powers,
What scents distinguish other lands from ours?

MELIBŒUS.

In English towns, these four the stranger choke:
Damp malt, machinery, gin, and sea-coal smoke.
Too much doth Paris in perfumery deal
Its native odor plainly to reveal:
But chocolate there prevails, upon the whole,
While musk and coffee mingle in Stamboul:
Rome with burnt wax and incense ever steams,
Something 'twixt violets and vanilla creams:
Florence enjoys a perfume all its own,
Of roasted chestnuts and the pine-tree's cone:
Malta breathes oranges across the deep,
To ships that hover nigh her castled steep:
Madrid in garlic doth all towns surpass:
New York is rich with gutters and with gas.

TITYRUS.

Ah! could I change for that aroma now
These hateful smells — this execrable cow,
The rank potato-fields, the pitchy pines,
These melons, withering on the wilted vines:
Fain would I change, for any stench of Art,
This mawkish Nature ——

MELIBŒUS.

Wherefore do you start?

TITYRUS.

What grateful steam along the corridor
Steals to my sense? and what persuasive roar?
Hark! 't is the dulcet thunder of the gong——

MELIBŒUS.

It speaks of seed-cakes, hyson and souchong:
Go, wretched TITYRUS! and get your tea;
Mine own is waiting in my cot for me.

VESPERS ON THE SHORE OF THE MEDITERRANEAN.

At Savona, a very ancient little city on the coast of Genoa, there stands a Madonna by the lighthouse, about twelve feet high, under which are inscribed, in letters of a corresponding size, two Sapphic verses, which are both good Latin and choice Italian — made by Gabriello Chiabrera, "the prince of Italian lyric poets," who was a native of Savona, —

> "In mare irato, in subita procella,
> Invoco te nostra benigna stella."

Valery, the most agreeable of Italian travellers, — a charming and instructive writer, and a pleasant corrective to the sharpness of Forsyth, — remarks that this pretty distich shows the genius and analogy of the two languages, the latter of which can only be well known to those who are conversant with the former.

These verses of Chiabrera's are actually sung, to this day, as the burden of an affecting litany to the Virgin, in daily use among the mariners of the Rivièra.

Religion's purest presence was not found,
By the first followers of our Saviour's creed,
In stately fanes where trump and timbrel-sound
Sent up the chorus in a strain agreed,
And where the decked oblation's wail might plead
For guilty man with Abraham's holy seed.

Not in vast domes, — horizons hung by men,
Where golden panels fret a marble sky,
And things below look up, and wonder when
Those life-like seraphim would start and fly!
Not where the heart is mastered by the eye
Will worship, anthem-winged, ascend most high.

But in the damp cathedral of the grove,
  Where Nature feels the sanctitude of rest,
Or in the stillness of the sheltered cove,
  Which noiseless water-fowl alone molest,
At times a reverence will pervade the breast
Which will not always come, a bidden guest.

Oft as the parting smiles of day and night
  Flush earth and ocean with a roseate hue,
And the quick changes of the magic light
  Prolong the glory of their warm adieu,
Each pilgrim on the hills, and every crew
On the lulled waters, frame their vows anew.

Then by the waves that lip Liguria's land,
  In Genoa's gulf, thou, wanderer! must have heard
What, more than hymns from Pergolesi's hand,
  The living soul of adoration stirred, —
And, like the note of Spring's first welcomed bird,
Some thoughts awoke — for which there is no word. —

The shipman's chant! as noting travellers tell,
  In either language — old and new — the same;
But more they might have truly said, and well,
  For 't is a speech the *universe* may claim;
Men of all times, all climes, and every name,
Devotion's tongue! which from the Godhead came.

HYMN.

Tost rudderless around the deep,
  By Apennine and Alpine blast,
Which o'er the surge in fury sweep,
  And make a bulrush of our mast,

We murmur in our half-hour's sleep,
To thee, Madonna! till the storm be past.
In mare irato, in subita procella,
Invoco te nostra benigna stella.

Whether for weeks our bark hath striven
With death in wild Sardinia's waves,
Or downward far as Tunis driven,
Threat us with life — the life of slaves;
We know whose hand its help has given,
And locked the lightning in its thunder caves.
In mare irato, in subita procella,
Invoco te nostra benigna stella.

O, Virgin! when the landsman's hymn,
At vesper time, on bended knee,
In sunlit aisle, or chapel dim,
Or cloister cell, is paid to thee,
Hear us! that ocean's pavement skim,
And join our anthem to the raging sea.
In mare irato, in subita procella,
Invoco te nostra benigna stella.

And when the tempest's wrath is o'er,
And tired Libeccio sinks to rest,
And starlight falls upon the shore
Where love sits watching, uncaressed,
Though hushed the tumult and the roar,
Again the prayer we 'll chant which Thou hast blest.
In mare irato, in subita procella,
Invoco te nostra benigna stella.

LOUISA'S GRAVE.

Deep in the city's noisy heart
  A sacred spot there lies;
Amid the tumult, yet apart,
  And shut from worldly eyes.

There, just beyond the chapel shade,
  Hid in a clovered mound,
Enough of innocence is laid
  To sanctify the ground.

Born, as the violets are, in May,
  With song of birds she came,
And when she sighed her soul away,
  The season was the same.

It seemed in heaven benignly meant
  To give this virgin birth
When all things beautiful are sent,
  To bless the budding earth.

But, if her birth befitted then
  The spring-time and the bloom,
Why, when that gladness came again,
  Why went she to the tomb?

O, let not impious grief accuse
  Kind Nature of a wrong!
Her form in flowers and fragrant dews
  Shall be exhaled ere long.

Her beauty was akin to them;
  Their elements combined
To shape the young, consummate stem,
  Whose blossom was her mind.

And now the blossom is with God;
  Soon shall the sun and showers
Wake from the slumber of the sod
  All that was ever ours.

No weary winter's frozen sleep,
  Under the torpid snows,
Her undecaying frame can keep
  In the clay's cold repose:

For all her mortal part shall melt,
  In other forms to rise,
Before her spirit shall have dwelt
  One summer in the skies.

A STORY OF THE CARNIVAL.

A NOBLE Austrian of Trieste
  Was wedded to as fair a creature
As e'er a bridal pillow blest;
Of all Vienna's court confessed
  The paragon, in form and feature.

Her husband, in his dog-star days, —
  I mean his youth's more sultry season, —
At galas, revels, routs and plays,
Had set full many a heart a-blaze,
  And blazed himself beyond all reason.

But, like a fire of pitchy wood,
  That rages for a while and flashes,
And suddenly becomes subdued,
Unless the resin is renewed,
  To a dull heap of sullen ashes:

Thus BARON STEINER'S fever-heat
  Seemed cooling to a quiet glimmer
Of bliss domestic and discreet:
More calmly now his pulses beat,
  Though age had made his eye no dimmer.

No more ecstatic glimpses now
  Of paradise, beneath a bonnet,

Warmed his imaginative brow;
No rosy lip inspired a vow,
  Nor angel's voice awoke a sonnet.

Pardon the Baron, then, I pray,
  You gentler readers of my story,
That, after long repose, one day
A humor seized him to be gay,
  Ere yet his whiskers had grown hoary.

CARNIVAL time was come at last:
  All Italy was filled with mummers;
Till Lent 't was held a sin to fast,
And winter days as fleetly passed
  As ever did a Tuscan summer's.

But, from Palermo to the Po,
  Such mirth, such masks, such feats of tennis,
Such revelry of high and low,
What bright metropolis could show
  As the proud spouse of ocean — Venice?

The gondolas that all night long
  Like fire-flies in July were glancing;
The games, the gladness and the throng
That rent the air with shout and song;
  The feasts, the drinking and the dancing:

The puppets and the strolling sights —
  With Punch, his wooden woman mauling;
The bridges hung with colored lights,
Like little rainbows, and the flights
  Of rockets, rushing, flashing, falling:

The flaming wheels, the whizzing snakes,
Soaring and lost among the Pleiads,
Then raining down in fiery flakes,
The deities of woods and lakes,
Fauns, Tritons, oreads, naiads, dryads:

The innumerable fry of fools,
Professional and *dilettanti;*
Jugglers, defying Nature's rules,
With monkeys too, and dancing mules
Graceful as pupils of PAPANTI.

All sorts of monsters — mermen, sharks —
Seals that could waltz and act genteelly;
Noah would have required two arks
For all the beasts that choked Saint Mark's,
Or clustered round the Campanile.

The peasant folk that thronged the square,
The dominos — a gaudy legion!
The comfit-sellers with their ware —
All these made merry Venice wear
The look of an enchanted region.

Since everything that 's rare or queer,
For which there neither name nor use is,
Was hither brought from far and near, —
Whatever in each hemisphere
Nature or man's quick brain produces.

And multitudes, all Europe through,
From far as Hungary and Poland,
Trooped hither — such a motley crew! —
Merely to mingle in and view
A pageant paralleled by no land.

Hither, with too much ease oppressed,
  Happy almost to melancholy,
The Baron speeds, a greedy guest,
To rest a while from too much rest,
  And dash life with a little folly.

But, lest his jealous dame might fret,
  He veiled the purpose of his going,
And whispered that he went to get,
In Brescia, payment of a debt
  Which some rich tenant there was owing.

"So, love, content thee for a while
  To live without a husband, lonely:
A week," he added, with a smile,
"Shall bring me back; ay, with a pile
  Of ducats for thy spending only."

Cheerfully then they bade farewell:
  The Baron hied aboard his galley;
She to her chamber's nun-like cell,
In solitary sort to dwell,
  With nothing male — nor cat, nor valet.

Hushed is the house; each vacant room
  Seems sacred to repose or illness;
So solemnly, as through the gloom
Of some new-opened Roman tomb,
  The sunlight falls upon the stillness.

But Leonore, — a neighbor by, —
  A widow, mischievous and silly,
Whose wanton spirit rose so high,
It overflowed each wicked eye,
  A restive, roguish, rampant filly;

About the gadding hour, came in,
  To feed her ear with such rare fuel
Of news as, who had lately been
Suspected of some private sin,
  And how some whispered of a duel:

And whether 't was a love affair,
  And what would be the consequences;
How Such-a-one had got a pair
Of twins; another lost her hair,
  And one her teeth, and one her senses.

And how that young phenomenon,
  Had such a wonderful contr'alto,
And how the Carnival went on,
And what disguise the meant to don,
  To flaunt in on the mad Rialto.

For all the world (at least, the best
  Half of it) was to Venice flocking,
And she was going with the rest;
To stay at home, in dull Trieste,
  Was most ridiculous — 't was shocking!

"Come, you shall join my party! Nay,
  Don't shake your head—I 'll take the scolding;
We 'll give to merriment one day,
And see such sights as you shall say
  'T were sin to live without beholding."

'T would take ten epics, numbering each
  Twelve books, to give a full narration
Of all the forms and modes of speech
She took to counsel, beg, beseech,
  And force the dame's determination.

She triumphed too ; that afternoon
   Saw them in their felucca skimming
The Adriatic's foam, and soon
They hoped amid the blue lagune
   To see the sea-born city swimming.

Meanwhile the Baron gayly flung
   Aside all thought of marriage duties;
Revelled the revellers among —
By day, grew youthful with the young —
   By night, unmasked Venetian beauties.

So flew a week — how brief are weeks
   To lawyers in their June vacation!
How fleeter far to him who seeks
From household cares, and female freaks
   And bores and bills, a relaxation!

The final night is come, and all
   Are flocking to the grand ridotto,
(Which means a sort of concert-ball)
Given in the gilt and Gothic hall
   Of the MARCHESA DI MINOTTO.

'T were a mad thing to try to light
   La Scala with a single taper;
But madder the attempt to write
The glories of that gaudy night
   On this poor single sheet of paper.

The myriad lamps, the brighter eyes,
   The music and the sweeter voices;
The ladies decked in gay disguise,
From whose angelic companies
   Young princes might have made their choices.

And Austria's Baron too was there;
His galliot in the stream was floating,
That, soon as morning blanched the air,
Homeward in haste he might repair,
To duller bliss his heart devoting.

Oft in the frenzy of the dance,
Amid the scene's intoxication,
He seemeth lost as in a trance;
A pouting lip, a sullen glance,
Flit o'er his dark imagination.

He dreams upon a wife in tears,
A month of sulkiness and sorrow;
A woman's wrath is in his ears,
His ecstasy is mixed with fears
Of his reception on the morrow.

But, lo! what wonder moves this way?
What meteor hath from heaven descended?
How light her limbs! — their airy play
Seems like the tossing of the spray!
At once his boding dream is ended.

Through many a minuet, on her,
Through Tyrol jig and Tarantella,
He gazes, but he cannot stir;
Still murmuring, as insane he were,
"Gesu! che brava! quanto bella!"

Anon, with beating heart and head,
Toward her amid the throng he presses;
"Fair lady, by your leave," he said,
"Together we 'll a measure tread;"
Blest man! her fingers he possesses.

He leads her forth; he whirls her through
  Waltz after waltz, till, growing dizzy,
She fain would sit — he seats him too;
One arm about her waist he drew,
  One hand was with her tresses busy.

"Nay, if you tease me, sir, good-night!"
  She rose in haste — and he rose with her;
"Farewell, sir; how in such a plight
I dread to meet my husband's sight!
  He knew not of my coming hither.

"And here I am, all lace and gold;
  Ah me! what madness was 't came o'er me!
How the dear soul would rave and scold,
These foolish trappings to behold,
  Should he perchance get home before me!"

"Nay, but I'll see you to the shore,"
  Quoth he; "these link-boys are so stupid."
To guide their way, a lad who bore
A lighted flambeau ran before,
  Fit representative of Cupid!

"'T is very dark and dangerous too —
  Here take my arm, *amico mio;*"
Thus toward the Grand Canal they drew
Where swiftly down the steps she flew,
  "Here is my gondola — Addio!"

With this, aboard she nimbly leaped,
  And hid within its curtained cover;
But ever close behind her kept,
And underneath, beside her crept,
  Her indefatigable lover.

The gondoliers, as off they bore
  The dame and her *inamorato*,
To cheer the labor of the oar
Struck up a chorus, as of yore
  They sang from the divine TORQUATO.

NOW TASSO'S lays are thrown aside,
  With Tyranny's neglected trophies;
And Venice, to her ocean-bride,
Even when the moon is on the tide,
  Repeats no more his tender strophes.

Perchance the pilgrim, wandering there,
  May hear some ballad, quaint or pretty,
Some silly words and foreign air,
Some modern trifle by AUBER,
  Or slight conceit of DONIZETTI:

But when romantic JOHNNY flies
  From his dull nook in smoky Britain,
He thinks beneath Italian skies
To hear each dog bark melodies,
  And music mewed by every kitten.

And when the Yankee cockney goes
  To Venice, on his virgin trip, he
Is apt, green sapling! to suppose
He shall hear sweeter strains than those
  That charmed him on the Mississippi.

But that 's a fallacy; for oft,
  On the Ohio, I have listened
To barcaroles so strangely soft,
That while at the rude words I scoffed,
  The moisture in mine eye has glistened.

And oftentimes the dulcet drone
  Of those queer, western river-catches
Moves a man more than he will own:
Such music I have seldom known
  As the poor negroes make at Natchez.

But, this digression to give o'er,
  The gondoliers howled forth a ditty,
And fast receded from the shore
Where Pleasure, but an hour before,
  Revelled, sole regent of the city.

Low in the west the sinking moon
  Gleamed faintly, looking wan and jaded;
And sadly, o'er the dark lagune,
Died the dead carnival's last tune,
  The carnival's last glimmer faded.

Afar a crimson lantern showed
  Where a small brigantine awaited
The coming of its final load;
Toward this with speed the boatmen rowed —
  The lady feared they were belated.

They reached the bark; the master cried,
  "Madam, for you alone we tarry;
The wind is brisk upon the tide — "
"For *me* alone! — no," she replied,
  "Since here are *two* of us to carry."

She climbed the deck; her faithful squire
  Lent her his hand, and followed after;
He knew her coyness soon must tire,
And for his insolent desire
  Read happy omens in her laughter.

O, yes — she smiled! he knew she would —
  In friendly mood they passed together
To the small cabin, where a brood
Of passengers, as best they could,
  Slept, snugly sheltered from the weather.

A drowsy scene! for all around,
  In spite of close, unsavory quarters,
Lay, fast in sweet oblivion bound,
And with harmonious noses drowned
  The gurgle of the sullen waters.

Close packed, as bees within a hive,
  Some nestled underneath the table;
Each nook, each angle was alive —
The berths were crammed, and four or five
  Lay cuddling round a coil of cable.

But through the swarm, with careful pace,
  O'er arms and legs, confusedly mingled,
Now o'er a foot and now a face
Stumbling, he found, by luck, one place
  Which none for their repose had singled.

"Be this thy couch to-night — this chest;
  Soon may the breathing of the billow
Rock thine exhausted limbs to rest!"
With this, her hand he gently pressed,
  Sank down, and made her lap his pillow.

Close at his side another dame,
  Hid in her mantle, was reposing,
From whom upon his weary frame
A sort of magnetism there came,
  His senses to a calm composing.

And nothing long his eyes could keep
  Free from that blessed seal of sorrow,
And care, and thought, and pleasure — sleep,
Sweet sleep! so perfect and so deep,
  As though there could be no to-morrow!

At last he woke to see the sun
  In at the open hatches peeping;
But his companions, every one,
As though their bliss were just begun,
  Lay still, their brains in Lethe steeping.

She, like the rest, indulged her nap;
  Hushed was the heart that lately fluttered,
Heedless of pleasure or mishap ——
But, "O! that this were BERTHA's lap,
  Or this were not my head!" he muttered.

Then curiosity — the vice
  First-born of womankind — came o'er him,
And half seduced him, once or twice,
To look upon this pearl of price
  That lay thus casketed before him.

And often, as his courage rose,
  He raised his hand, but straight withdrew it; —
There 's something sacred in repose,
Even in an after-dinner doze;
  One fears too rudely to break through it.

Deep, deep in happy dreams she lies!
  Now might he gaze on her securely;
He lifts her mask — at once her eyes
Fasten on his: "Great Heaven!" he cries,
  "How like! — how like! — *'t is* BERTHA, surely!"

His BERTHA's laugh disturbed the snore
  Of the veiled heap of dormant matter
That lay beside him, on the floor;
She threw her cloak off — LEONORE!
  He gazed in palsied horror at her.

"O, for a storm!" he thought; "a squall!
  Breakers! or but a burst of thunder!
O! that a water-spout would fall!
Or aught that might this jade appal,
  And keep her soul of mischief under!"

But Jove consented to the jest;
  Widow and wife would have their laughter;
And, ere the vessel touched Trieste,
All was forgiven and all confessed,
  And Peace dwelt with them ever after.

ADDRESS,

WRITTEN FOR THE OPENING OF THE BOSTON THEATRE, IN FEDERAL-STREET.

Behind this mystic veil, that, newly-furled,
Unfolds your true to our ideal world,
The actors wait, like mariners on deck,
Watching afar their country's misty speck,
Till, near enough to catch the welcome bell,
The breath of gardens and the pine's warm smell,
At once they mark the filmy vapor soar,
And rood by rood reveal the sacred shore:
Thus have we watched, until the screen ascends,
Disclosing home again and troops of friends,
Every loved smile and well-remembered face,
Each reverend landmark in its ancient place,
The light-house there of yonder nameless eyes,
And the gray peaks that round the distance rise.

Joy to the city! from whose triple mount
Transplanted Learning struck her earliest fount,
Where the twin daughters of the Drama came
Ere yet our nation had achieved a name,
And reared for England's genius and our own
A fitting stage, a perdurable throne,

Which time and dulness have assailed in vain,
Fashion's light swarm and Zeal's ascetic train.
All evil auguries have been fulfilled,
All the bad cry of calumny is stilled,
The liberal sunshine of reviving Taste
From our glad heaven each wintry sign hath chased,
The maledictions too benignly showered,
And all the clouds upon our house that lowered.

When the sad Sisters, wandering exiled thence,
Bade the reformer's promised reign commence,
Though many a pitying breast and eyelid here
Deigned a kind sigh and dropped a useless tear,
He took his triumph, proud even such to win,
But desolation had before him been.
As Moscow's victors, dumb with wondering awe,
Rode through the gates, but nothing living saw;
By fort and church and vacant palace passed,
But heard no drum, nor gun, nor bugle blast,
Nor fierce defiance answering from the roofs
The measured beating of their horses' hoofs, —
Thus did the new possessor and his hordes
Grimly profane the silence of our boards,
With wanton hand the mysteries unfold,
And rend the caverns where our thunders rolled;
No ghost opposed him on his impious track,
No Roman soldier bade the invader back;
Weapons there were, but all of men bereft:
Whole heaps of fasces, — not a lictor left.
So through the solitude that quelled his fear
The exulting zealot held his wild career,

Tore from its wonted niche the hallowed bust,
And laid the Prince of Poets in the dust,
Whose gloomy shade, still hovering round the fane,
Wandered a beggar in his own domain,
Like great Ulysses on the sullen shore
That knew his footstep and his face no more.

Say, now, to whom our brief defeat was due,
The strict precisian, or in part to you?
Patrons, to you this half-reproof we owe,
He called it conquest not to find a foe;
The victims we of Friendship's fickle whim,
By you deserted, not subdued by him.
Long had we marked the fatal reign advance
Of Ethiop song and spectacle and dance,
Majestic thought in grovelling words was drowned,
Words poor in sense, but silvered o'er with sound;
From Prospero's hand the rod and volume fell,
No spirits came nor recognized the spell,
But serious lovers of our art disdained
A shrine like Egypt's even by beasts profaned,
Where dogs and drunkards, into service prest,
Pleased a dull pit, and gave the gods a jest.

O, many a true and fond believer then
Kept his old faith, but kept it hid from men;
Oft from the shelf took down the tragic tome,
And conned his Hamlet, unreproved, at home.
But who had heart, when thus the Drama sank,
Amid the champions of her cause to rank?
Even we, her servants, faithful to the last,
Owned her doom just, as she to judgment passed, —

Guilt on her brow, confusion in her eye,
All the more low for having soared so high.

Less, then, the austere morality we blame,
That came, and saw, and bought, and overcame;
Cold as the blast from Caucasus, that brings
The plague-smit Orient health upon its wings,
The storm assailed us, but its icy breath
Purged the sick atmosphere from seeds of death,
And gave our clime, for languor and disease,
Strength and glad life again, and smiles like these.

But let no sour disciple of the school
That deems the bard a mere melodious fool;
Let no gaunt leader of the cynic tribe,
No cold-eyed pharisee, nor solemn scribe,—
Censorious Catos, that, like him of old,
Naught in refinement but its vice behold,
And, aping him, would banish, in their hate,
These "Attic babblers" that corrupt the state,—
Let no such bigot hope to lord it long
O'er the chief realm of passion and of song,
Or think that Sabine harshness to revive
Which on spare lentils kept itself alive!

Rather let us from Scipio's gentler mind
Learn wiser truths and precepts more refined;
Nor in meet season one calm hour refuse
To the mild service of the lettered muse;
But to the poet and the player accord
The praise which merit counts its best reward;

That, if new Garricks, on Missouri's banks,
Or other Kembles, earn a nation's thanks,
They may not, boasting of their triumphs there,
Upbraid our barren soil and kindless air,
And say of us—'Twas but a sordid age;
They had no poet, and despised the stage.

JUNE 30, 1846.

A SONG FOR SEPTEMBER.

SEPTEMBER strews the woodland o'er
  With many a brilliant color;
The world is brighter than before —
  Why should our hearts be duller?
Sorrow and the scarlet leaf,
  Sad thoughts and sunny weather,
Ah me! this glory and this grief
  Agree not well together.

This is the parting season — this
  The time when friends are flying;
And lovers now, with many a kiss,
  Their long farewells are sighing.
Why is earth so gayly drest?
  This pomp that autumn beareth
A funeral seems, where every guest
  A bridal garment weareth.

Each one of us, perchance, may here,
  On some blue morn hereafter,
Return to view the gaudy year,
  But not with boyish laughter:
We shall then be wrinkled men,
  Our brows with silver laden,
And thou this glen mayst seek again,
  But nevermore a maiden!

Nature perhaps foresees that Spring
  Will touch her teeming bosom,
And that a few brief months will bring
  The bird, the bee, the blossom;
Ah! these forests do not know —
  Or would less brightly wither —
The virgin that adorns them so
  Will never more come hither!

LEYDEN GLEN, GREENFIELD.

PROEM TO MANZONI'S "CINQUE MAGGIO;"*

INSCRIBED TO MARY RUSSELL MITFORD.

I.

Read what the Christian poet saith,
  O lady! in my faithful rhyme,
Of the great Captain and his death;
  And venerate, with me, that Faith
Which in the aspiring man of crime,
  Whom gentle goodness must abhor, —
Who carried into every clime
  The fury and the waste of war, —
Some seeds of pardon can discern;
Yea, from his dying pillow learn
A lesson worthy of the solemn strain
That long as all his triumphs shall remain.

II.

Him and his history of blood,
  Him and the ruin that he made,
By Moskwa's and the Nile's far flood,
  All his bad victories, displayed
On many an arch and boastful pile
That wake the wandering Briton's smile,

* See page 118.

To find no name of England there:
These can the lenient Muse recall,
And breathe forgiveness over all,
With a majestic prayer.

III.

Child of his time, the poet speaks
Such thoughts as to the time belong—
No more his private malice wreaks
In the small vengeance of a song:
That day of doom—that bitter day,
When Hate sate sov'ran o'er his lay,
And bade him, in his burning line,
To an eternal curse consign
God's universe—hath passed away.

IV.

For, men who seem to shape their age,
Yea, fashion history to their will,
And on Fame's perdurable page
Write their own record, good or ill,—
Even these, if rightly scanned,
Are but the ivory toys upon the board
Moving, to lose or win,
By force of mitre, crown or sword,—
Yet all their little leaps have been
Directed by a wiser hand!

V.

Therefore the gracious Lombard muse, benign
Interpreter of Rome,

Finds in this Attila one spark divine,
  That hath in heaven its home:
So welcomes him to his eternal rest!
With such high music as befits the blest.

VI.

Not so the grave Etrurian lyre
  Had sounded, in that sterner age
When vengeance thrilled the quivering wire,
When what the poet thought was fire —
  And what he said was rage:
When the great Ghibeline, gloomy and unsparing,
Moved like Fate's shadow, at his girdle wearing
Peter's lent keys — the while his iron hand
Held Pluto's passport to the sunless land!

VII.

He, to these images of wrong
  Wherewith his unforgiving heart
Peopled the pitiless realm of his dark song —
To Dionysius and his tyrant throng*
  Had added Bonaparte:
And with the rest of that fell brood,—
  Pyrrhus, and Òbizzo the fair,
  And the grim Paduan with the raven hair, —
  Had sunk him in that river of despair,
To drink his fill of blood.

* Dante, in the twelfth Canto of the Inferno, describes the tyrants who outraged humanity as plunged in a river of boiling blood, while Centaurs gallop about the stream, shooting them with arrows. Among these sinners he numbers Attila, Dionysius, Òbizzo of Este, and Ezzelino the tyrant of Padua.

VIII.

But He that, in the midst of wrath,
  Remembers mercy still,
Reveals by Calvary a path
  Conducting out of ill,
Into the glad, immortal fields above,
Where His great justice is allayed by Love.
Be this our trust: and may the lofty bard
  Who rules the Latin minstrelsy to-day
Soften within us what is harsh or hard.
    Here calumny should cease —
  Peace for the weary soldier let us pray,
  Since by that lone and lowly death-bed lay
    His cross — who was the Prince of Peace.

MANZONI'S ODE

ON THE DEATH OF NAPOLEON,

(THE FIFTH OF MAY.)

He was: and motionless in death,
As that unconscious clay,
Robbed of so mighty breath,
In speechless ruin lay,
Even so, bewildered, stunned, aghast,
Earth at the tale is dumb,
Pondering the final agonies
Of him, the man of fate,
And wondering when, with tread like his,
Again to desolate
Her trampled fields, all dust and blood,
A mortal foot shall come.

Him, upon his refulgent throne,
In silence could my soul survey,
And when, by varying fortunes blown,
He fell, rose — fell again and lay,
My spirit to the million's tone
Echoed back no reply;
Virgin alike from servile praise,
And cowardly abuse;
But now, as wane the meteor's rays,
I let my genius loose,
To fall upon his urn one strain
Perchance that shall not die.

IN MORTE DI NAPOLEONE,

(IL CINQUE MAGGIO.)

Ei fu; siccome immobile,
Dato il mortal sospiro,
Stette la spoglia immemore
Orba di tanto spiro,
Cosí percossa, attonita,
La terra al nunzio sta;
Muta pensando all' ultima
Ora dell'uom fatale,
Nè sa quando una simile
Orma di piè mortale
La sua cruenta polvere
A calpestar verrà.

Lui sfolgorante in soglio
Vide il mio genio e tacque,
Quando con vece assidua
Cadde, risorse, e giacque,
Di mille voci al sonito
Mista la sua non ha:
Vergin di servo encomio
E di codardo oltraggio
Sorge or commosso al subito
Sparir di tanto raggio,
E scioglie all'urna un cantico,
Che forse non morrà.

From the Alps to the Pyramids,
  From the Manzanar to the Rhine,
He tracked his eagles, as the bolt
  Follows its flashing sign.
From Tanais to Scylla glancing,
  From the West to the Eastern brine:
Was this true greatness? — That high doom
  Let after times declare;
We to the Greatest bow, from whom
  He held so large a share
Of the Most High, creative mind,
  Stamped by the hand divine.

The tremulous, tempestuous joy
  Of lofty enterprise — the heart
That knew no rest from its employ,
  But burned to play the imperial part;
And won and kept a prize whose dream
    Had madness seemed, at best —
All he had proved and passed — renown
  That after danger brightest smiled,
Defeat and flight, and victory's crown,
  A ruler now, and now exiled, —
  Twice humbled in the dust, defiled,
    Twice at the altar blest.

Two ages, 'gainst each other armed,
  Him for their umpire named,
Looking on him as Fate: he charmed
  To silence their contentions — tamed
Their frantic feuds, and sat supreme
    Their factious rage above:

Dall' Alpi alle Piramidi,
Dal Mansanare al Reno,
Di quel securo il fulmine
Tenea dietro al baleno;
Scoppiò da Scilla al Tanai,
Dall' uno all' altro mar.
Fu vera gloria ? ai posteri
L' ardua sentenza; nui
Chiniam la fronte al Massimo
Fattor, che volle in lui
Del creator suo spirito
Più vasta orma stampar.

La procellosa e trepida
Gioja d' un gran disegno,
L' ansia d' un cor, che indocile
Ferve pensando al regno,
E 'l giunge, e tiene un premio
Ch' era follia sperar,
Tutto ei provò ; la gloria
Maggior dopo il periglio,
La fuga, e la vittoria,
La reggia, e il triste esiglio,
Due volte nella polvere,
Due volte su gli altar.

Ei si nomò : due secoli,
L' un contro l' altro armato,
Sommessi a lui si volsero
Come aspettando il fato:
Ei fe' silenzio, ed arbitro
S' assise in mezzo a lor;

He vanished — and his vacant days
  Spent in so small a sphere!
Majestic mark for envy's gaze,
  And pity most sincere —
For unextinguishable hate,
    And never-vanquished love.

As on the shipwrecked seaman's head
  The o'erwhelming breakers pour,
Beyond whose foaming fury spread
  Around him and before,
The wretch had vainly gazed to see
    The intangible, far strand:
Thus o'er that strong but sinking soul
  Swept Memory's whelming tide,
As oft his actions to enrol
  In Fame's re'cords he tried; —
But from the everlasting scroll
    Fell, faint, his harassed hand.

O! at the silent, dying hour
  Of some dull day of rest,
His lightning eyes in sullen lower,
  And his arms folded on his breast,
How often have his days of power
    Rushed on remembrance thick!
Then to his backward-roving thought
  The moving tents, the trench, the course,
The gleaming squadrons have been brought,
  The sea-like surging of the horse,
The martial word, the swift command,
    The obedience, no less quick.

Ei sparve, e i dì nell' ozio
Chiuse in sì breve sponda,
Segno d' immensa invidia,
E di pietà profonda,
D' inestinguibil odio,
E d'indomato amor.

Come sul capo al naufrago
L' onda s' avvolve e pesa,
L' onda su cui del misero
Alta pur dianzi e tesa
Scorrea la vista a scernere
Prode remote invan;
Tal su quell' alma 'l cumulo
Delle memorie scese;
Oh! quante volte ai posteri
Narrar se stesso imprese,
E sulle eterne pagine
Cadde la stanca man!

Oh! quante volte al tacito
Morir d' un giorno inerte,
Chinati i rai fulminei,
Le braccia al sen conserte,
Stette, e dei dì che furono
L' assalse il sovvenir.
Ei ripensò le mobili
Tende, e i percossi valli,
E il lampo dei manipoli.
E l' onda dei cavalli,
E il concitato imperio,
E il celere obbedir.

Alas! at such an overthrow
   Haply that panting spirit failed;
Haply despairing drooped: but, lo!
   The Omnipotent from heaven hailed
His child, and unto purer air,
      With pitying hand conveyed;
And through the flowery paths of hope
   Dismissed him to the eternal fields,
Where more than even his lofty scope
   Perfect fruition yields,
And where the glory that hath past
      Is silence now, and shade.

Beneficent, immortal, fair,
   Faith holds her wonted triumph yet:
Write this besides: Rejoice! for ne'er
   Did haughtier potentate forget
His pride, and meekly bow at last,
      To Golgotha's disgrace.
Thou, o'er his weary dust, each low
   Calumnious word forbear;
The God from whom afflictions flow,
   All comfort and all care,
Beside him deigned, on his low bed,
      To find a resting-place.

Ahi! forse a tanto strazio
  Cadde lo spirto anelo;
  E disperò; ma valida
  Venne una man dal cielo,
  E in più spirabil aere
  Pietosa il trasportò;
    E l' avviò su i floridi
    Sentier della speranza,
    Ai campi eterni, al premio
    Che i desiderii avanza,
    Ov' è silenzio e tenebre
    La gloria che passò.

Bella, immortal, benefica
  Fede ai trionfi avvezza,
  Scrivi ancor questo; allegrati:
  Che più superba altezza
  Al disonor del Golgota
  Giammai non si chinò.
    Tu dalle stanche ceneri
    Sperdi ogni ria parola;
    Il Dio che atterra e suscita,
    Che affanna e che consola,
    Sulla deserta coltrice
    Accanto a lui posò.

HUDSON RIVER.

Rivers that roll most musical in song
  Are often lovely to the mind alone;
The wanderer muses, as he moves along
  Their barren banks, on glories not their own.

When, to give substance to his boyish dreams,
  He leaves his own, far countries to survey,
Oft must he think, in greeting foreign streams,
  "Their names alone are beautiful, not they."

If chance he mark the dwindled Arno pour
  A tide more meagre than his native Charles;
Or views the Rhone when summer's heat is o'er,
  Subdued and stagnant in the fen of Arles;

Or when he sees the slimy Tiber fling
  His sullen tribute at the feet of Rome,
Oft to his thought must partial memory bring
  More noble waves, without renown, at home;

Now let him climb the Catskill, to behold
  The lordly Hudson, marching to the main,
And say what bard, in any land of old,
  Had such a river to inspire his strain.

Along the Rhine, gray battlements and towers
  Declare what robbers once the realm possessed ;
But here Heaven's handiwork surpasseth ours,
  And man has hardly more than built his nest.

No storied castle overawes these heights,
  Nor antique arches check the current's play,
Nor mouldering architrave the mind invites
  To dream of deities long passed away.

No Gothic buttress, or decaying shaft
  Of marble, yellowed by a thousand years,
Lifts a great landmark to the little craft —
  A summer cloud! that comes and disappears.

But cliffs, unaltered from their primal form
  Since the subsiding of the deluge, rise
And hold their savins to the upper storm,
  While far below the skiff securely plies.

Farms, rich not more in meadows than in men
  Of Saxon mould, and strong for every toil,
Spread o'er the plain, or scatter through the glen,
  Bœotian plenty on a Spartan soil.

Then, where the reign of cultivation ends,
  Again the charming wilderness begins;
From steep to steep one solemn wood extends,
  Till some new hamlet's rise the boscage thins.

And these deep groves forever have remained
  Touched by no axe — by no proud owner nursed:
As now they stand they stood when Pharaoh reigned,
  Lineal descendants of creation's first.

Thou Scottish Tweed, a sacred streamlet now!*
  Since thy last minstrel laid him down to die,
Where through the casement of his chamber thou
  Didst mix thy moan with his departing sigh;

A few of Hudson's more majestic hills
  Might furnish forests for the whole of thine,
Hide in thick shade all Humber's feeding rills,
  And darken all the fountains of the Tyne.

Name all the floods that pour from Albion's heart,
  To float her citadels that crowd the sea,
In what, except the meaner pomp of Art,
  Sublimer Hudson! can they rival thee?

* "As I was dressing, on the morning of Monday, the 17th of September, Nicolson came into my room, and told me that his master had awoke in a state of composure and consciousness, and wished to see me immediately. I found him entirely himself, though in the last extreme of feebleness. His eye was clear and calm; — every trace of the wild fire of delirium extinguished. 'Lockhart,' he said, 'I may have but a minute to speak to you. My dear, be a good man; — be virtuous, — be religious, — be a good man. Nothing else will give you any comfort when you come to lie here.' He paused, and I said, 'Shall I send for Sophia and Anne?' — 'No,' said he; 'don't disturb them. Poor souls! I know they were up all night. God bless you all!' With this he sunk into a very tranquil sleep, and, indeed, he scarcely afterwards gave any sign of consciousness, except for an instant on the arrival of his sons. They, on learning that the scene was about to close, obtained a new leave of absence from their posts; and both reached Abbotsford on the 19th. About half past one, P. M., on the 21st of September, Sir Walter breathed his last, in the presence of all his children. It was a beautiful day, — so warm that every window was wide open, and so perfectly still that the sound of all others most delicious to his ear — the gentle ripple of the Tweed over its pebbles — was distinctly audible, as we knelt around the bed; and his eldest son kissed and closed his eyes." — LOCKHART'S LIFE OF SIR WALTER SCOTT.

Could boastful Thames with all his riches buy,
  To deck the strand which London loads with gold,
Sunshine so bright — such purity of sky —
  As bless thy sultry season and thy cold ?

No tales, we know, are chronicled of thee
  In ancient scrolls ; no deeds of doubtful claim
Have hung a history on every tree,
  And given each rock its fable and a fame.

But neither here hath any conqueror trod,
  Nor grim invaders from barbarian climes ;
No horrors feigned of giant or of god
  Pollute thy stillness with recorded crimes.

Here never yet have happy fields laid waste,
  The ravished harvest and the blasted fruit,
The cottage ruined, and the shrine defaced,
  Tracked the foul passage of the feudal brute.

" Yet, O Antiquity ! " the stranger sighs,
  " Scenes wanting thee soon pall upon the view ;
The soul's indifference dulls the sated eyes,
  Where all is fair indeed — but all is new."

False thought ! is age to crumbling walls confined ?
  To Grecian fragments and Egyptian bones ?
Hath Time no monuments to raise the mind,
  More than old fortresses and sculpturèd stones ?

Call not this new which is the only land
  That wears unchanged the same primeval face
Which, when just dawning from its Maker's hand,
  Gladdened the first great grandsire of our race.

Nor did Euphrates with an earlier birth
   Glide past green Eden towards the unknown south,
Than Hudson broke upon the infant earth,
   And kissed the ocean with his nameless mouth.

Twin-born with Jordan, Ganges, and the Nile!
   Thebes and the pyramids to thee are young;
O! had thy waters burst from Britain's isle,
   Till now perchance they had not flowed unsung.

THE FEUD OF THE FLUTE-PLAYERS.*

AN ANCIENT ROMAN BALLAD, RECENTLY DISCOVERED.

Before the war with old Tarentum, twenty years or thereabout,
When the city dwelt serenely, wealth within and peace without;
When the temple-doors of Janus seemed once more about to close,
Suddenly among the people here in Rome a feud arose.

* "Another transaction of this year I should pass over as trifling, did it not seem to bear some relation to religion. The flute-players, taking offence because they had been prohibited by the last censors from holding their repasts in the temple of Jupiter, which had been customary from very early times, went off in a body to Tibur; so that there was not one left in the city to play at the sacrifices. The religious tendency of this affair gave uneasiness to the senate; and they sent envoys to Tibur to endeavor that these men might be sent back to Rome. The Tiburtines readily promised compliance, and, first calling them into the senate-house, warmly recommended to them to return to Rome; and then, when they could not be prevailed on, practised on them an artifice not ill adapted to the dispositions of that description of people: on a festival day, they invited them separately to their several houses, apparently with the intention of heightening the pleasure of their feasts with music, and there plied them with wine, of which such people are always fond, until they laid them asleep. In this state of insensibility they threw them into waggons, and carried them to Rome: nor did they know anything of the matter, until, the waggons having been left in the Forum, the light surprised them, still heavily sick from the debauch. The people then crowded about them, and, on their consenting at length to stay, privilege was granted them to ramble about the city in full dress, with music, and the license which is now practised every year during three days. And that license which we see practised at present, and the right of being fed in the temple, were restored to those who played at the sacrifices." — Livy, *Book IX.*

Quintus Barbula was consul — but the cause the gods concerned,
More than that for which the palace of King Priamus was burned.

Thus it was: the censor Appius passed a damnable decree,
That the Flute-Players (an order slightly prized by such as he),
When the sacrifice was over, from the temple should depart,
Nor, upon the relics feasting, thus profane their sacred art:
From the days of Numa downward, this their privilege had been;
Never till the bigot Appius was the custom deemed a sin.
Frequent came the jovial suppers, where the consecrated wine
Moistened many a dainty fragment, juicy, tender, and divine,—
Many a sweet-bread fat and holy, such as Umbria's pasture yields,
Flanks that once beside Clitumnus roved among the Tuscan fields,
Livers lifted from the altar, free from blemish, fair and sound,
Tasting of the blessed omens which the sage Haruspex found.
Soon as the majestic Flamen with his priests had left the fane,
Such delicious morsels tempted Jove's musicians to remain.

Now the Appian law is published, posted on the temple-gates,
Sadly each musician spells it, sadly eyes his drooping mates;
"No more feasting, no more drinking! what shall give us heart to play?"
Mournfully to one another every visage seemed to say:
"'T was the perquisites that mainly paid the labor of our lungs,
Steaming chines and ribs delicious, roasted loins and luscious tongues.
Taking these away is taking from the journeyman his hire,
From the ox his wonted fodder, and the fuel from the fire:
Could the flute so sweetly warble, save our breath inspired the holes?
As to flutes our breath is needful, so the supper to our souls."

Grumbling thus, they called a council, o'er some Sabine dull and dead,
In a tap-room by the Tiber, at the sign of "Tarquin's Head."

There the veteran, Corellus, dark as Agamemnon, rose,
Sternly silent, for a moment — then unfolded thus his woes:
"Brothers! unto whom our mistress, crowned Euterpe, gave the skill
By a touch to call Elysium from your ebon tubes at will,
Fill your beechen goblets brimming, vile although this liquid be.
Drink 'Despair to censor Appius!' deeply drink, then list to me.
August comes, the thirsty August, and the holidays are nigh,
When to Jove, a guiltless offering, must the annual heifer die;
When from every town in Latium all the pious rustics throng,
Mingling with our lofty concert and the sacred smoke their song;
How without our aid, inform me, can the festival proceed?
Vainly must the wine be lavished, vainly must the victim bleed;
Come, we 'll teach these niggard Romans unto us how much they owe;
Never till we quit the city will the fools our value know.
I for one, like Caius Marcius, here abjure my native land;
Follow me, ye gallant minstrels! me, the leader of your band!
Let 's to Antium or to Tibur — if our country shake us off,
Well I know the men of Tibur Phœbus' children will not scoff:
But by Pan! the god of shepherds and the father of the flute,
While among this thankless people, from this moment I am mute."

All the Flute-Players assented; all, upon the following day,
Gathered in the busy Forum — whispered, but forbore to play.
Boys and women muttered round them, "Why are our musicians dumb?
Why, as though their lips were palsied, and their magic fingers numb?
Come, Sirs! play the march of Tullus; or Virginia's funeral dirge;
Give us now 'The Gauls are coming;'" thus their various choice they urge;
Till, unmoved by prayers or curses, from the tumult they retreat,
Hissed and hooted from the Forum, scowling down the sacred street.

Silent walked the lone procession,— old Corellus went the first,—
Doggedly and slowly marching, with their instruments reversed.
None could guess their secret counsel, though the reason well they knew
Why the discontented minstrels thus in dumb disdain withdrew.
Ev'n as at the games assembled, oft the young spectators grieve,
If the clouds in black battalions gathering o'er them they perceive,
Watch with troubled eyes the welkin, fearing lest the tempest's wrath
Deluging the wide arena, turn the circus to a bath;
Thus as from the city's portal toward the hills the players passed,
Every little child was mourning, every virgin's face o'ercast.

All the citizens with sorrow saw depart the sullen troop,
Knowing well, for want of music, how the festival must droop;
Shook his head the solemn augur; "Evil auspices!" quoth he;
"Wanting music, what libation to the gods can grateful be?
Heaven is always hard of hearing, when the lips alone beseech:
Harps and lyres and flutes were given us, to exalt our earthly speech;
Speech we use among each other, to our horses and our hounds,
But the dwellers on Olympus only hear harmonious sounds."

Therefore to the Sabine senate certain envoys promptly went,
Praying that the renegados duly homeward might be sent.
Thus the Tiburtines gave answer (Rome and they were friendly then),
"Though of old ye stole our women, we 'll not rob you of your men;
Tell the Fathers and the Flamen, ere the fires begin to burn,
Ere the sacred rite commences, the deserters will return."
Then the messengers departed; straightway the performers all
By the herald's voice were summoned to the ancient council-hall,
Where the gravest and the gayest of the ruling elders prayed
Earnestly that Rome's petition by her sons might be obeyed;
Lest their festival should languish, and the gods with evil eye
Mark the joyless adoration and the tuneless pageantry.

But in vain the placid spokesman argued with the stubborn crew,
"Never!" cried the stout Corellus; "'t is in vain the people sue;
Though the pontiff and the consuls, though the Capitolian rock,
Hither crawling, should implore us, their petition I would mock;
Starve us, would they? frugal Romans! let the thrifty censor then
Take from Jupiter his fatling — let him offer heaven a hen;
Haply to the son of Saturn, the supremely great and good,
Fish and eggs, and simple pot-herbs, may not prove unwelcome food."
Thus the embassy they flouted, while the senate smiling said,
"'T were inhospitable surely to refuse our friends a bed;
Since persuasion cannot stir them, here with us they must remain:
Let them here assist our worship; Latium's loss is Tibur's gain."

Now the holidays in Tibur on the morrow would begin,
One day sooner than the custom with the Romans aye had been;
And the Flute-Players had promised in the public place to play
All their most melodious measures, amorous, and sad, and gay —
Phrygian marches, Pyrrhic hornpipes, all the new Athenian airs, —
That the town should swear was never music to be matched with theirs;
While the Tiburtines, in secret, laid among themselves a plan
To return the tuneful strangers ere the Roman rites began.
So upon the joyous morrow, when the sacrifice was o'er,
And the players had indulged them till their finger-ends were sore,
When the matrons and the damsels one by one the square forsook,
Every gentleman in Tibur to his house a minstrel took.

Proud was every hungry piper to be made a noble's guest;
Gladly, after so much blowing, tasted the delight of rest.
Singly and in pairs they scattered here and there about the town,
Couched and revelled at the banquet, poured the potent pledges down;

Well they paid their morning's labor, deeply drank and largely fed,
Better wine they found in Tibur than was sold at "Tarquin's Head."

Soon as every vanquished artist, tumbling from the festive board,
Heavy with his wine and slumber, on the marble pavement snored,
Careful hands conveyed them quickly, and as gently as they could,
Toward the market, where some wine-carts, waiting for them, empty stood;
Snugly in the straw they laid them, sweetly dozing, side by side,
"Forward to the seven-hilled city, march!" the merry townsmen cried;
So, by star-light, after nightfall, from the Latin Gate they start;
"Tibur to the Romans, Greeting;" this was writ on every cart.

Not till daybreak did the tumbrils at the Colline Port arrive;
Only dogs and early swallows, and the sentry, seemed alive.
"Wherefore," growled the guard, unknowing what within the litter lay,
"Wherefore bring your carrion hither? — trow ye 't is a market-day?
Gods! if this were told the censor, little cause ye 'd have to grin!"
"Beasts for Jupiter," they answered, tittering as they entered in.
Straight they took them to the forum; there they left them till the sun,
Peeping o'er Mount Esquilinus, might arouse them, one by one.

Rose the town betimes that morning; toward the Forum swarmed the boys;
Trumpets brayed and crashed the cymbals — all was merriment and noise;
Farmers with their wives and daughters, mariners from Ostia's port,
Scarlet caps and Alban jackets, gathering to the place of sport.
Soon the voices and the sunshine woke the pale and haggard crew,
Sick and feverish, faint and shivering with the chillness of the dew.

Round about with temples throbbing, aching and bewildered eyes,
Long they gazed, and on each other stared with idiot-like surprise.
Little did the crowd's derision and their own wild looks explain
How they came there, what the cause was of their paleness and their
pain.
Each, that he had supped in Tibur, would his very lungs have staked;
How then was it that in Latium, in the Forum there, they waked?

Then the populace, delighted with the jest, to vex them more,
Brought a lying vintner forward, who "by Vesta's altar" swore
He had seen them all carousing there in Rome the night before;
While another knave pretended to have met them, loose of tread,
Reeling homeward after midnight from the sign of "Tarquin's Head."
Shame forbade all further question: "Naught but that vile tavern's
juice,"
Cried Corellus, "such confusion in our senses could produce."
Musing, toward the fane they hastened, and with more than wonted
art
Stirred the fountains of devotion in the whole assembly's heart;
Never in Apulia's orchards did the nightingales of June
Gurgle forth so dulcet anthems to the stillness of the moon;
And the censor in his wisdom, just beginning to suspect
How by fast and thin potations minstrelsy and mirth are checked,
Ruled that thrice a month the players might a solemn supper hold,
Thrice a year, in full procession, march in crimson clad and gold:
So the famous Feud was ended, and the secret long was kept,
How they woke within the Forum, who in Tibur's town had slept.

GHETTO DI ROMA.

"Sol chi non lascia eredità d 'affetti
Poca gioia ha dell 'urna." — UGO FOSCOLO.

WHOEVER, led by worship of the past,
Or love of beauty, even in its wane,
Wastes a sweet season of delightful sadness
In wandering mid the wilderness of Rome,
May see — as I did, many a summer since —
A wretched quarter of the sacred city,
Where the poor dregs of Israel's children dwell.

'T is called *the Ghetto*, and the pious townsman
Shuns it, unless his piety lie deep
Enough to teach him not to turn aside
From any form of human brotherhood:
Hard by the muddy Tiber's idle flow,
Beyond the shadow of the Vatican,
Yet within sound, almost, of choirs that chant
Morning and evening to a Christian organ,
Its prison-like and ragged houses rise.
A miry street leads through the unholy realm,
Where no saint's chapel, perfect in proportion,
Breaks the long ugliness with one fair front;

Nor ever open door breathes odorous fumes
Of silver censers on the passers by.
Here hymns are never heard, nor sacring bell,
Nor benediction from benignant lips,
Nor whispered aves to the cold-eyed Virgin.
The cowled procession brings no tapers here,
With crucifix and banner-bearing boys,
To take the taint out of the Hebrew air.

At either entrance of the ill-paved way
A gate as massive as the Scæan was,
And grim as that through which the Tuscan passed
On his dread journey to the fires of hell,
Swings on its hinges till the set of sun,
And then is bolted till he glare again.
Thus dawn and night to the poor captives come
Made by the barring only and unbarring
Of the spiked portals; for the blessed ray
Pierces no lattice, gilds no threshold here.
The gloomy shops a mingled steam exhale
Of withered greens, and musty grocers' ware,
And such rank offal as the meaner sort
Of curs will mumble when their lent seems long.
Here at high noon the petty trade proceeds
By the dim tallow which the greasy counter
Receives in minted drops, — the only coin,
Save that of oaths, which is abundant here.

It chanced that — anno urbis conditæ —
Some time 'twixt Romulus and Gregory —
A noble youth, upon a summer's eve,
Pressed through the Ghetto, towards the Capitol;

And glancing upward in his hasty walk,
Saw at a window, looking sadly down,
A maiden brighter than the vesper star,
Already lighted in the purple heaven.
He marked the star, and knew the hour was late;
He heard the bell that warned the lagging stranger
The time was come for Christians to be gone;
But he remained, still walking to and fro,
Gazing on her, who frowned not at his gaze.
The smirched mechanic at his sill was sitting,
The noise of gossips at the corner rose,
The broker left his shop, the scribe his supper,
And publican and pharisee came forth
To chat of profit in the dusky light;
A jargon filled the air, — the gates were shut.

Thus was the noble Roman for the night
Locked in ignoble durance; yet can beauty
Transmute the common soil from which it springs
To sands of gold — the Ghetto seemed Golconda.
To him, the hovel where that jewel shone
Appeared a Persian palace. Underneath
The radiant window where she sat enshrined,
Her father — a gross cub of Reuben's tribe —
Kept a small wine-shop where his brother sots
Cheered the dull nights with cups of sour Velletri.
'T was not an inn, — he did not furnish beds,
Save what his guests beneath his tables found.
Yet, entering here, the gentle stranger plied
The housekeeper with solid arguments
For shelter till the morning. Judas melted;
The ducats won him — like his ancestor,

Who sold his soul, he would have sold his daughter,
Could he have done so, — for a piece of silver.

Yet let no stain upon the virgin fall;
The young patrician found in her a pearl
Such as the husband of Lucretia had.
She yielded to his love, but not his longing,
And in a week became the Roman's wife.
What scandal now among the gentry flies!
Still 'mid the most unbridled raging fastest,
For calumny's ill fire, so quick to catch,
Kindleth most readily the lightest tinder.
'T is epicurean too, and loves to prey
On dainty victims, — turns from base defects,
To gorge on blemishes in better blood.

This lover, who, descending from his birth,
Both birth and creed had stained by such a choice,
Was the best scion of an ancient house,
Whose name — Corsini — was the Pontiff's own.
The sinless regent of the Lateran
Expostulated, scolded, fretted, fumed, —
'T was mentioned, privately, he swore a little, —
For cursing is a papal perquisite:
But anger's fury is no match for love's —
His last dread weapon, excommunication,
Was launched in vain, — his graceless nephew laughed,
Repaid the scoffs of his compeers with scorn,
And with his wife, more dear to him than sceptres,
Fled to his castle near the sea, not far
From the frontier of Naples, — shining Anxur.
There, wholly happy in her love, he dwelt

Almost forgetful of the world beyond,
Save when at times, to make his home still dearer,
In his felucca, o'er the summer ocean,
He sailed with her to gay Parthenope.
But brief their absence, — each was heaven to each,
And pleasure vainly wooed them to a brighter.
In games and gardening, — sports in wood and field,
Books and the sweet companionship of song, —
Smoothly their silken web of life was woven,
And the seven hills lived only in remembrance.

Now the sad passage of my story comes.
The duke was forth upon the hills a hunting;
The boar was famous, — they had tracked him long, —
The terror of the hills, — the shepherd's dream:
A beast like that which in thy market-place
Stands, my dear Florence! ugly and of brass.
Full hard the lordly huntsman pressed his game,
And swiftly bounding, with a careless leap, —
His hot veins dancing, full of ruddy life, —
Hallooing, glowing, cheering on his riders,
And thinking more of danger to the boar
Than his own safety, — at a sudden turn,
The faithless joint of his o'er-labored steed
Failed him, — he stumbled, and his lord was thrown.
"Breathe on me, Rachel! — Bear me to my lady!"
Were the sole words his bloodless lips could murmur;
His spine was broken, and his Rachel saw him
Borne homeward, hanging like a vacant sack
On some poor mule returning from the mill.

The castle dates its ruin from that day:
Grief in the hall makes trouble in the hamlet, —

The manor sickened in its master's loss,
Thrift and content and plenty fled the village,
Which seemed joint widow with its weeping lady.
But when 'tis stormy weather in the south,
The sunshine laughs upon the northern hills,
And the same rain that beats one harvest down
Gives fulness, joy and ripeness, to another.
Distance makes music of discordant sounds,
As heard afar the town's confusing roar
Turns to a hum that lulls the Dryad's ear.

Thus to the hearing of the wolf of Rome
Came the glad tidings of his kinsman's death,
For the dull wail that thrilled the Apennine
Changed to rejoicing as it reached St. Peter's.
Low on his knees the grateful sovereign knelt,
And thanked the Almighty for so just a judgment:
His counsellors, cool, meditative men,
Spurred on his own opinion, and agreed
'Twere lenity most criminal to spare
The guilty cause and partner of such sin.
So by a savage edict, such as Herod,
That king in Jewry, might have blushed to utter,
The lands and fastnesses of fallen Corsini,
Orchards, woods, meads, and all the herds therein,
Were seized, and confiscated to the See.
But, since the estate had been so long polluted,
The interdiction of the church was added,
That none should dwell there, save unwholesome things —
The daily lizard and the nightly owl,
And the lean foxes of Maremma's fen.
So the fields pined, — the stagnant vapor spread

From green Pontina, poisoning all the air,
And Love's bright region grew a wilderness.

But for the woman — what became of her?
The papal Switzers, with unpitying hands,
Tore her babes from her, — thrust her from the chamber
Which upon earth had been her land of promise,
And happy haven of fulfilment too,
And, spitting on her as upon a scorpion,
Bade her go crawl upon her knees to Rome,
Become a Christian, and implore that Virgin,
Of whose own stock her Hebrew fathers came,
To pardon her that she was born a Jewess.

So barefoot, faint, frenzied with fear and sorrow,
She followed those rough pikemen of the Pope,
Till their steeds bore them from her aching sight.
And still she walked, for many a sultry day,
Bleeding, and dampening with continual drops
Of anguish and fatigue, from eyes and pores
Gushing unchecked, the pestilential path
That marks the marshes with a line of dust.
A crust thrown at her from a passing cart
Was all her sustenance, save the bitter scum
Skimmed from the puddles where she slaked her thirst;
Yet scarce she halted till the cupola
Rose in the distance like a part of heaven,
The inner vault of the sky's double dome, —
'Twas her own city — yet her enemies'!

Closed was the gate, — the gate of St. Sebastian, —
So early was it when she reached the walls;

And, sinking on the grass, she slept till dawn.
Soon as the sentinel, with punctual hand,
Hung up the keys and took his carbine down,
And ere the drowsy casements were unfolded,
She plodded on, through streets well known of old,
Towards the dull Ghetto and her father's house.
But you — O, you, whose fancies only paint
Delightful pictures, and from gay romance
Have heard the pleasure of return, — the bliss
Of happy children meeting with their parents, —
And all the raptures of revived affections,
Shift now imagination's helm a little;
Indulge no vision of a loved repentant,
Forgiven and smiling at a father's hearth.
But see, instead, the lady of a duke,
The titled mother of two Christian boys,
Thrust from her delicate repose of life,
Where servants, the vaunt-couriers of her wishes,
Nursed her fastidious affluence of comfort,
Into that noisome burrow of the Jews,
Amid the filth and want and rough disuse
Of all the courtesies and gentle customs
That ring with velvet tires the wheels of life.

But this she could have borne; all this was nothing
To the rude greeting of an envious race
Who called her recreant — gloried in her downfall,
Jeered the soiled remnants of her silk attire,
And, wittily malignant, oft contrasted
Her jewelled fingers with her bleeding feet.
Yet, lest the holy Father, in his wrath,
Might think it meet to drag her from this den,

And plunge her in some worse one of his own,
Here, half in pity, half in punishment,
Was she concealed and from the daylight barred,
Fed with rank bits and beaten like a drudge;
Till Reason, sapped by inly gnawing fears
Of her poor children's fate, and stunned, as 't were,
By that vast fall from blessedness to bondage,
Reeled from its throne, and left her lunatic.
So to the dungeon for the mad they haled her,
And chained her soft limbs 'mid the rotten straw,
Wet with white froth from a dead maniac's lips.
But some sweet angel stole her sense away,
And nothing knew she of the jailer's lash;
For with her mind her feeling too had fled,
The very fountain of her tears was frozen.
Dumbly she nestled there — a thing of ice —
Until she melted, like a drop of dew,
Into the sunshine and the air of heaven.
'T was whispered, then, that by the Pope's command
Her two fair boys were burnt, — and 't was believed, —
For in that time the church was famed for rigor.

But 't was a fiction, — many years ago,
Amid the galley-slaves together chained,
Who delve all day the rubbish of the Forum,
And keep the channel of the Tiber free,
Two haggard men were fettered, leg to leg,
Who still in company walked, worked and rested,
Like the twin monster-brothers of Siàm.
They too were brothers, — by their fellow-slaves
One was called Bàrabbas and one Iscariot.
I saw them once in Caracalla's Baths, —

Their white teeth glaring from their idiot faces,
And Folly shining in their snaky eyes!
Few knew their story; but 't was told to me
With their true name, — their true name was Corsini.

THE SHADOW OF THE OBELISK.

——— combien d'hommes ont regardé cette ombre
en Egypte et à Rome ? CHATEAUBRIAND.

HOMEWARD turning from the music which had so entranced my brain
That the way I scarce remembered to the Pincian Hill again, —
Nay, was willing to forget it underneath a moon so fair,
In a solitude so sacred, and so summer-like an air, —
Came I to the side of Tiber, hardly conscious where I stood,
Till I marked the sullen murmur of the venerable flood.

Rome lay doubly dead around me, sunk in silence calm and deep :
'T was the death of desolation — and the nightly one of sleep.
Dreams alone, and recollections, peopled now the solemn hour,
Such a spot and such a season well might wake the Fancy's power :
Yet no monumental fragment, storied arch or temple vast,
Mid the mean, plebeian buildings loudly whispered of the Past.

Tethered by the shore, some barges hid the wave's august repose ;
Petty sheds of humble merchants nigh the Campus Martius rose :
Hardly could the dingy Thamis, when his tide is ebbing low,
Life's dull scene in colder colors to the homesick exile show.
Winding from the vulgar prospect, through a labyrinth of lanes,
Forth I stepped upon the Corso where its greatness Rome retains.

Yet it was not ancient glory, though the midnight radiance fell
Soft on many a princely mansion, many a dome's majestic swell ;

Though, from some hushed corner gushing, oft a modern fountain gleamed,
Where the marble and the waters in their freshness equal seemed:
What though open courts unfolded columns of Corinthian mould?
Beautiful it was — but altered! naught bespake the Rome of old.

So, regardless of the grandeur, passed I towards the Northern Gate;
All around were shining gardens — churches glittering, yet sedate;
Heavenly bright the broad enclosure! but the o'erwhelming silence brought
Stillness to mine own heart's beating, with a moment's truce of thought,
And I started as I found me walking, ere I was aware,
O'er the Obelisk's tall shadow, on the pavement of the square.

Ghost-like seemed it to address me, and conveyed me for a while,
Backward, through a thousand ages, to the borders of the Nile;
Where, for centuries, every morning saw it creeping, long and dun,
O'er the stones perchance of Memphis, or the City of the Sun.
Kingly turrets looked upon it — pyramids and sculptured fanes;
Towers and palaces have mouldered, but the shadow still remains.

Out of that lone tomb of Egypt, o'er the seas the trophy flew;
Here the eternal apparition met the millions' daily view.
Virgil's foot has touched it often — it hath kissed Octavia's face —
Royal chariots have rolled o'er it, in the frenzy of the race,
When the strong, the swift, the valiant, mid the thronged arena strove,
In the days of good Augustus, and the dynasty of Jove.

Herds are feeding in the Forum, as in old Evander's time;
Tumbled from the steep Tarpeian all the towers that sprang sublime.

Strange! that what seemed most inconstant should the most abiding
prove;
Strange! that what is hourly moving no mutation can remove:
Ruined lies the cirque! the chariots, long ago, have ceased to roll—
Even the Obelisk is broken—but the shadow still is whole.

What is Fame! if mightiest empires leave so little mark behind,
How much less must heroes hope for, in the wreck of humankind!
Less than even this darksome picture, which I tread beneath my feet,
Copied by a lifeless moonbeam on the pebbles of the street;
Since, if Cæsar's best ambition, living, was to be renowned,
What shall Cæsar leave behind him, save the shadow of a sound?

UPON A LADY, SINGING.

Oft as my lady sang for me
That song of the lost one that sleeps by the sea,
Of the grave on the rock, and the cypress tree,
Strange was the pleasure that over me stole,
For 't was made of old sadness that lives in my soul.

So still grew my heart at each tender word,
That the pulse in my bosom scarcely stirred,
And I hardly breathed, but only heard:
Where was I? — not in the world of men,
Until she awoke me with silence again.

Like the smell of the vine, when its early bloom
Sprinkles the green lane with sunny perfume,
Such a delicate fragrance filled the room:
Whether it came from the vine without,
Or arose from her presence, I dwell in doubt.

Light shadows played on the pictured wall
From the maples that fluttered outside the hall,
And hindered the daylight — yet, ah! not all;
Too little for that all the forest would be, —
Such a sunbeam she was, and is, to me!

When my sense returned, as the song was o'er,
I fain would have said to her, "Sing it once more,"
But soon as she smiled my wish I forbore:
Music enough in her look I found,
And the hush of her lip seemed sweet as the sound.

TO A LADY,

WITH A HEAD OF POPE PIUS NINTH.

My gift went freighted with a hope, —
Slight bark upon a doubtful sea!
Yet, under convoy of the Pope,
Successful may the venture be;
For thus good Pius whispered me,
"Mi fili, Benedicite!"

His blessing now I will transfer
To thee, although I hardly know
What Latin form appropriate were, —
"Cor meum!" — shall I call thee so?
No, let the learned language be
But, sweetheart, Benedicite!

Your cardinals are blooming yet,
Pride of the brook! the meadow's gem!
So, ere his sun be wholly set,
I send, in due return for them,
The Pope — hark, love, he says to thee,
"My daughter, Benedicite!"

O, take his blessing then, — for ne'er
Did evil come from holy touch;
A righteous man's effectual prayer,
As the Saint says, availeth much, —
So, for this once, a Papist be,
Nor scorn his Benedicite!

STANZAS.

"We are such stuff as dreams are made of."

I.

We have forgot what we have been,
  And what we are we little know;
We fancy new events begin,
  But all has happened long ago.

II.

Through many a verse life's poem flows,
  But still, though seldom marked by men,
At times returns the constant close;
  Still the old chorus comes again.

III.

The childish grief, the boyish fear,
  The hope in manhood's breast that burns;
The doubt, the transport and the tear,
  Each mood, each impulse, oft returns.

IV.

Before mine infant eyes had hailed
  The new-born glory of the day,
When the first wondrous morn unveiled
  The breathing world that round me lay:

V.

The same strange darkness o'er my brain
  Folded its close, mysterious wings,
The ignorance of joy or pain,
  That each recurring midnight brings.

VI.

And oft my feelings make me start,
  Like footprints on some desert shore,
As if the chambers of my heart
  Had heard their shadowy step before.

VII.

So, looking into thy fond eyes,
  Strange memories come to me, as though
Somewhere—perchance in Paradise—
  I had adored thee long ago.

TO A LADY,

WITH A HEAD OF DIANA.

My Christmas gifts were few — to one
  A fan, to keep love's flame alive,
Since even to the constant sun
  Twilight and setting must arrive.

And to another — she who sent
  That splendid toy, an empty purse —
I gave, though not for satire meant,
  An emptier thing — a scrap of verse.

For thee I chose Diana's head,
  Graved by a cunning hand in Rome,
To whose dim shop my feet were led
  By sweet remembrances of home.

'T was with a kind of pagan feeling
  That I my little treasure bought, —
My mood I care not for concealing, —
  "Great is Diana!" was my thought.

Methought, howe'er we change our creeds,
  Whether to Jove or God we bend,
By various paths religion leads
  All spirits to a single end.

The goddess of the woods and fields,
  The healthful huntress, undefiled,
Now with her fabled brother yields
  To sinless MARY and her child.

But chastity and truth remain
  Still the same virtues as of yore,
Whether we kneel in Christian fane
  Or old mythologies adore.

What though the symbol were a lie,—
  Since the ripe world hath wiser grown,—
If any goodness grew thereby,
  I will not scorn it for mine own.

So I selected DIAN's head
  From out the artist's glittering show;
And this shall be my gift, I said,
  To one that bears the silver bow.

To her whose quiet life has been
  The mirror of as calm a heart;
Above temptation from the din
  Of cities, and the pomp of art.

Who still hath spent her active days
  Cloistered amid her happy hills,
Not ignorant of worldly ways,
  But loving more the woods and rills.

And thou art she to whom I give
  This image of the virgin queen,
Praying that thou, like her, mayst live
  Thrice blest! in being seldom seen.

STEUART'S BURIAL.

The bier is ready and the mourners wait,
The funeral car stands open at the gate.
Bring down our brother; bear him gently, too;
So, friends, he always bore himself with you.
Down the sad staircase, from the darkened room,
For the first time, he comes in silent gloom:
Who ever left this hospitable door
Without his smile and warm "good-bye," before?
Now we for him the parting word must say
To the mute threshold whence we bear his clay.

The slow procession lags upon the road, —
'T is heavy hearts that make the heavy load;
And all too brightly glares the burning noon
On the dark pageant — be it ended soon!
The quail is piping and the locust sings, —
O grief, thy contrast with these joyful things!
What pain to see, amid our task of woe,
The laughing river keep its wonted flow!
His hawthorns there — his proudly-waving corn —
And all so flourishing — and so forlorn!
His new-built cottage, too, so fairly planned,
Whose chimney ne'er shall smoke at his command.

Two sounds were heard, that on the spirit fell
With sternest moral — one the passing bell!
The other told the history of the hour,
Life's fleeting triumph, mortal pride and power.
Two trains there met — the iron-sinewed horse
And the black hearse — the engine and the corse!
Haste on your track, you fiery-wingèd steed!
I hate your presence and approve your speed;
Fly! with your eager freight of breathing men,
And leave these mourners to their march again!
Swift as my wish, they broke their slight delay,
And life and death pursued their separate way.

The solemn service in the church was held,
Bringing strange comfort as the anthem swelled,
And back we bore him to his long repose,
Where his great elm its evening shadow throws, —
A sacred spot! There often he hath stood,
Showed us his harvests and pronounced them good;
And we may stand, with eyes no longer dim,
To watch new harvests and remember him.

Peace to thee, Steuart! — and to us! the All-Wise
Would ne'er have found thee readier for the skies:
In His large love He kindly waits the best,
The fittest mood, to summon every guest;
So, in his prime, our dear companion went,
When the young soul is easy to repent:
No long purgation shall he now require
In black remorse — in penitential fire;
From what few frailties might have stained his morn
Our tears may wash him pure as he was born.

EPITAPH UPON MY FRIEND, DAVID STEUART ROBERTSON.

From his grave-stone at Lancaster.

Here Steuart sleeps: and should some brother Scot
Wander this way, and pause upon the spot,
He need not ask, now life's poor show is o'er,
What arms he carried, or what plaid he wore:
So small the value of illustrious birth,
Brought to this solemn, last assay of earth!
Yet, unreproved, his epitaph might say
A royal soul was wrapt in Steuart's clay,
And generous actions consecrate his mound,
More than all titles, though of kingly sound.

TO A LADY.

IN RETURN FOR A BOOK OF MICHEL ANGELO'S SONNETS.

> "Non ha l'ottimo artista alcun concetto
> Ch' un solo marmo in se non circoscriva
> Col suo soverchio, — e solo a quello arriva,
> La man' che obbedisce all intelletto."
>
> *Sonnetto di Michel Angelo Buonarroti.*

No master artist e'er imagines aught
That lies not hid, awaiting mortal gaze,
In the rough marble, — if but fitly wrought
By one whose hand his intellect obeys:
His magic touch the stone's white silence wakes,
And, lo! the god from his long bondage breaks:

Breaks like the blue morn from an orient vapor,
Which made the pilgrim doubtful of the day;
Or like the music from the written paper
O'er which some poet lets his fancy play;
Like new-born April from the winter's tomb,
Or any joy that springs from any gloom.

Lady! the fair material of our being
Is put before us, to be carved at will:
O! wisely work, with clear conception seeing
The perfect shape that shall reward thy skill:
Something there may be, cut from every life,
Something to worship — whether saint or wife.

Learn Patience first; for Patience is the part
 Of all whom Time records among the great,
The only gift I know, the only art,
 To strengthen up our frailties to our fate:
Through long endurance comes the martyr crown
That makes the hero blush for his renown.

And, as by many steps, from thorn to flower,
 The patient petals of the rose recover
The hues and fragrance of the golden hour,
 That saw last summer's nightingale her lover,
So may thy soul, if constancy be thine,
Toil on through trials till it dawn divine!

SLEEP.

Somnus — or Morpheus was his name ?
I have forgot — I cannot keep
My schoolboy learning : as it came,
It went — I mean the god of sleep.

That god and I were once fast friends,
But now his face I seldom see ;
More oft the blessed rain descends
In Egypt, than his dews on me.

Ah me ! the joy I had in dreams —
The nightly comfort to forget —
Is mine no more ; the morning beams
On eyes like faded asters, wet :

Yes, moistened oft with poisonous tears,
Till the burnt lashes look so few,
You might suppose that threescore years
Were mine, instead of thirty-two !

Well, I can wait a little more,
A little longer wake and weep,
Until the welcome grave restore
The bliss of an unbroken sleep.

Let me remember Him that while
  His tired disciples round him slept —
(The sinless born, that knew no guile !) —
  Watched in Gethsemane, and wept.

AUGUST, 1851.

SONNET.

BY BUONAGIUNTA DA LUCCA.

This reade is rife, that oftentime
Great climbers fall unsoft:
  In humble dales is footing fast,
The trode is not so tickle,
  And though one fall through heedless haste,
Yet is his miss not mickle.

SPENSER.

WHAT man, by chance, is up, on Fortune's wheel,
  Let him not triumph in his being high;
For when her smiling side she doth reveal,
  Then she turns round, and, golden days, good-bye!

Never was meadow of so fresh a green,
  Nor ever had such flowers as would not fade;
And Nature's law in everything is seen,
  That what was highest must be lowest laid.

Therefore, let him who wears to-day the crown
  Be modest in his joy — 't is mickle pain
From the top-stair of all to tumble down;
  But every mountain cometh to a plain.

BIRTH-PLACE OF ROBERT BURNS.

A lowly roof of simple thatch, —
   No home of pride, of pomp, and sin, —
So freely let us lift the latch,
   The willing latch that says, "Come in."

Plain dwelling this! a narrow door —
   No carpet by soft sandals trod,
But just for peasant's feet a floor, —
   Small kingdom for a child of God!

Yet here was Scotland's noblest born,
   And here Apollo chose to light;
And here those large eyes hailed the morn
   That had for beauty such a sight!

There, as the glorious infant lay,
   Some angel fanned him with his wing,
And whispered, "Dawn upon the day
   Like a new sun! go forth and sing!"

He rose and sang, and Scotland heard —
   The round world echoed with his song,
And hearts in every land were stirred
   With love, and joy, and scorn of wrong.

Some their cold lips disdainful curled;
  Yet the sweet lays would many learn;
But he went singing through the world,
  In most melodious unconcern.

For flowers will grow, and showers will fall,
  And clouds will travel o'er the sky;
And the great God, who cares for all,
  He will not let his darlings die.

But they shall sing in spite of men,
  In spite of poverty and shame,
And show the world the poet's pen
  May match the sword in winning fame.

SORRENTO.

MIDWAY betwixt the present and the past —
  Naples and Pæstum — look! Sorrento lies:
Ulysses built it, and the Sirens cast
  Their spell upon the shore, the sea, the skies.

If thou hast dreamed, in any dream of thine,
  How Paradise appears, or those Elysian
Immortal meadows which the gods assign
  Unto the pure of heart — behold thy vision!

These waters, they are blue beyond belief,
  Nor hath green England greener fields than these:
The sun — 't is Italy's; here winter's brief
  And gentle visit hardly chills the breeze.

Here Tasso dwelt, and here inhaled with spring
  The breath of passion and the soul of song.
Here young Boccacio plumed his early wing,
  Thenceforth to soar above the vulgar throng.

All charms of contrast — every nameless grace
  That lives in outline, harmony, or hue —
So heighten all the romance of the place,
  That the rapt artist maddens at the view,

And then despairs, and throws his pencil by,
  And sits all day and looks upon the shore
And the calm ocean with a languid eye,
  As though to labor were a law no more.

Voluptuous coast! no wonder that the proud
  Imperial Roman found in yonder isle
Some sunshine still to gild Fate's gathering cloud,
  And lull the storm of conscience for a while.

What new Tiberius, tired of lust and life,
  May rest him here to give the world a truce,—
A little truce from perjury and strife,
  Justice adulterate and power's misuse?

Might the gross Bourbon — he that sleeps in spite
  Of red Vesuvius ever in his eye,
Yet, if he wake, should tremble at its light,
  As 't were Heaven's vengeance, promised from on high, —

Or that poor gamester, of so cunning play,
  Who, up at last, in Fortune's fickle dance,
Aping the mighty in so mean a way,
  Makes now his dice the destinies of France, —

Might they, or any of Oppression's band,
  Sit here and learn the lesson of the scene,
Peace might return to many a bleeding land,
  And men grow just again, and life serene.

ON THE DEATH OF DANIEL WEBSTER.

TWENTY-FOURTH OF OCTOBER, 1852.

Comes there a frigate home? what mighty bark
  Returns with torn, but still triumphant sails?
Such peals awake the wondering Sabbath — hark!
  How the dread echoes die among the vales!

What ails the morning, that the misty sun
  Looks wan and troubled in the autumn air?
Dark over Marshfield! — 't was the minute gun:
  God! has it come that we foreboded there?

The woods at midnight heard an angel's tread;
  The sere leaves rustled in his withering breath;
The night was beautiful with stars; we said,
  "This is the harvest moon," — 't was thine, O Death!

Gone, then, the splendor of October's day!
  A single night, without the aid of frost,
Has turned the gold and crimson into gray,
  And the world's glory, with our own, is lost.

A little while, and we rode forth to greet
  His coming with glad music, and his eye
Drew many captives, as along the street
  His peaceful triumph passed, unquestioned, by.

Now there are moanings, by the desolate shore,
  That are not ocean's; by the patriot's bed,
Hearts throb for him whose noble heart no more —

Break off the rhyme — for sorrow cannot stop
  To trim itself with phrases for the ear, —
Too fast the tears upon the paper drop:

Fast as the leaves are falling on his bier,
  Thick as the hopes that clustered round his name,
While yet he walked with us, a pilgrim here.

He was our prophet, our majestic oak,
  That, like Dodona's, in Thesprotian land,
Whose leaves were oracles, divinely spoke.

We called him giant, for in every part
  He seemed colossal; in his port and speech,
In his large brain and in his larger heart.

And when his name upon the roll we saw
  Of those who govern, then we felt secure,
Because we knew his reverence for the law.

So the young master * of the Roman realm
  Discreetly thought, we cannot wander far
From the true course, with Ulpian at the helm.

But slowly to this loss our sense awakes;
  To know what space it in the forum filled,
See what a gap the temple's ruin makes!

* Alexander Severus.

Kings have their dynasties, but not the mind;
  Cæsar leaves other Cæsars to succeed,
But Wisdom, dying, leaves no heir behind.

Who now shall stand the regent at the wheel?
  Who knows the dread machinery? who hath skill
Our course through oceans unsurveyed to feel?

Her mournful tidings Albion lately sent,
  How he, the victor in so many fields,
Fell, but not fighting, in the fields of Kent;

The chief whose conduct in the lofty scene
  Where England stood up for the world in arms,
Gave her victorious name to England's queen.

But peaceful Britain knows, amid her grief,
  She could spare now the soldier and his sword;
What can our councils do without our chief?

Blest are the peace-makers! — and he was ours, —
  Winning, by force of argument, the right
Between two kindred, more than rival powers.

The richest stones require the gentlest hand
  Of a wise workman — be our brother's faults,
For all have faults, by wisdom gently scanned.

Resume the rhyme, and end the funeral strain;
  Dying, he asked for song, — he did not slight
The harmony of numbers, — let the main
  Sing round his grave great anthems, day and night.

The autumn rains are falling on his head,
  The snows of winter soon will shroud the shore,
The spring with violets will adorn his bed,
  And summer shall return, — but he, no more!

We have no high cathedral for his rest,
  Dim with proud banners and the dust of years;
All we can give him is New England's breast
  To lay his head on, — and his country's tears.

NOVEMBER 1ST, 1852.

DREAMS.

Some certain space of every life,
  Benignly 'twas decreed by Heaven,
However hot or hard the strife,
  Must be to dreams and slumber given.

Ah! once this wise, benignant law,
  Fool that I was! I did not know;
And thought him doltish when I saw
  Pale Prudence to his chamber go:

And said, "If life be any boon,
  'T is surely disregard of God
To lose in sleep these stars, this moon —
  Did He make moonlight for a clod?

And, in my pride of heart, methought
  I will not sleep —— am I a Turk?
Therefore I sat and read and wrought,
  For my vain study seemed like work.

But now, in middle age, I find
  The gray hairs ripening, and I say
What profit was it, if my mind
  Got wealth, — but threw the world away?

175

When my heart flutters late at night,
   When my head swims at early morn,
I count my gains, — and find them light,
   Poor fancies! that were best unborn.

Then do I know that, after all,
   The law prevails, — for still it seems,
When my night labor I recall,
   That work of mine — it was but dreams!

TO JAMES RUSSELL LOWELL,

IN RETURN FOR A TALBOTYPE PICTURE OF VENICE.

POET and friend! if any gift could bring
A joy like that of listening while you sing,
'T were such as this, — memorial of the days —
When Tuscan airs inspired more tender lays;
When the gray Apennine, or Lombard plain,
Sunburnt, or spongy with autumnal rain,
Mingled perchance, as first they met your sight,
Some drops of disappointment with delight;
When, rudely wakened from the dream of years,
You heard Velino thundering in your ears,
And fancy drooped, — until Romagna's wine
Brought you new visions, thousand-fold more fine;
When first in Florence, hearkening to the flow
Of Arno's midnight music, hoarse below,
You thought of home, and recollected those
Who loved your verse, but hungered for your prose,
And more than all the sonnets that you made,
Longed for the letters — ah, too poorly paid!

Thanks for thy boon! I look, and I am there;
The soaring belfry guides me to the square;
The punctual doves, that wait the stroke of one,
Flutter above me and becloud the sun;

'T is Venice! Venice! and with joy I put
In Adria's wave, incredulous, my foot;
I smell the sea-weed, and again I hear
The click of oars, the screaming gondolier.
Ha! the Rialto — Dominic! a boat;
Now in a gondola to dream and float:
Pull the slight cord and draw the silk aside,
And read the city's history as we glide;
For strangely here, where all is strange, indeed,
Not he who runs, but he who swims, may read.
Mark now, albeit the moral make thee sad,
What stately palaces these merchants had!
Proud houses once! — Grimani and Pisani,
Spinelli, Foscari, Giustiniani;
Behold their homes and monuments in one!
They writ their names in water, and are gone.
My voyage is ended, all the round is past, —
See! the twin columns and the bannered mast,
The domes, the steeds, the Lion's wingèd sign,
"Peace to thee, Mark! Evangelist of mine!" *

Poetic art! reserved for prosy times
Of great inventions and of little rhymes;
For us, to whom a wisely-ordering Heaven
Ether for Lethe, wires for wings, has given;
Whom vapors work for, yet who scorn a ghost,
Amid enchantments disenchanted most;
Whose light, whose fire, whose telegraph had been
In blessed Urban's liberal days a sin,

* The legend of the winged Lion of Saint Mark, seen everywhere, at Venice — "Pax tibi, Marce! Evangelista meus."

Sure, in Damascus, any reasoning Turk
Would count your Talbotype a sorcerer's work.

Strange power! that thus to actual presence brings
The shades of distant or departed things,
And calls dead Thebes or Athens up, or Arles,
To show like spectres on the banks of Charles!
But we receive this marvel with the rest;
Nothing is new or wondrous in the West;
Life 's all a miracle, — and every age
To the great wonder-book but adds a page.

SAINT PERAY.

ADDRESSED TO H. T. P.

When to any saint I pray,
It shall be to Saint Peray.
He alone, of all the brood,
Ever did me any good:
Many I have tried that are
Humbugs in the calendar.

On the Atlantic, faint and sick,
Once I prayed Saint Dominick:
He was holy, sure, and wise;—
Was 't not he that did devise
Auto da Fès and rosaries?—
But for one in my condition
This good saint was no physician.

Next, in pleasant Normandie,
I made a prayer to Saint Denis,
In the great cathedral, where
  All the ancient kings repose;
But, how I was swindled there
  At the "Golden Fleece,"—he knows!

In my wanderings, vague and various,
  Reaching Naples — as I lay
  Watching Vesuvius from the bay,
I besought Saint Januarius.
But I was a fool to try him;
Naught I said could liquefy him;
And I swear he did me wrong,
Keeping me shut up so long
In that pest-house, with obscene
Jews and Greeks and things unclean —
What need had I of quarantine?

In Sicily at least a score, —
In Spain about as many more, —
And in Rome almost as many
As the loves of Don Giovanni,
Did I pray to — sans reply;
Devil take the tribe! — said I.

Worn with travel, tired and lame,
To Assisi's walls I came:
Sad and full of homesick fancies,
I addressed me to Saint Francis;
But the beggar never did
Anything as he was bid,
Never gave me aught — but fleas, —
Plenty had I at Assise.

But in Pròvence, near Vaucluse,
  Hard by the Rhone, I found a Saint
Gifted with a wondrous juice,
  Potent for the worst complaint.

'T was at Avignon that first —
In the witching time of thirst —
To my brain the knowledge came
Of this blessed Catholic's name;
Forty miles of dust that day
Made me welcome Saint Peray.

Though till then I had not heard
Aught about him, ere a third
Of a litre passed my lips,
All saints else were in eclipse.
For his gentle spirit glided
With such magic into mine,
That methought such bliss as I did
Poet never drew from wine.

Rest he gave me, and refection, —
Chastened hopes, calm retrospection, —
Softened images of sorrow,
Bright forebodings for the morrow, —
Charity for what is past, —
Faith in something good at last.

Now, why should any almanack
The name of this good creature lack?
Or wherefore should the breviary
Omit a saint so sage and merry?
The Pope himself should grant a day
Especially to Saint Peray.
But, since no day hath been appointed,
On purpose, by the Lord's anointed,
Let us not wait — we 'll do him right;
Send round your bottles, Hal — and set your night.

FRANCESCA DA RIMINI.

A PICTURE BY ARY SCHOEFFER.

You restless ghosts that roam the lurid air,
I feel your misery, — for I was there:
Yes, I myself, here breathing and alive,
Have seen the storm, and heard the tempest drive
Yet while the sleet went, withering as it past,
And the mad hail gave scourges to the blast,
While all was black below, and flame above,
Have thought — 't is little to the storm of Love:
You know that sadly, know it to your cost,
Ah, too much loving, and forever lost!

Still, suffering spirits! ev'n your doom affords
Kisses and tears, however poor in words;
Brief is your story, but it liveth long —
O! thank for that your poet and his song:
Be it some comfort, in that hateful Hell,
You had a lover of your love to tell;
One that knew all — the ecstasy, the gloom,
All the sad raptures that precede the tomb;
The fluttering hope, the triumph and the care, —
The wild emotion, and the sure despair.

Not every friend hath friendship's finer touch,
To pardon passion, when it mounts too much;

Not every soul hath proved its own excess,
And feared the throb it still would not repress;
But he whose numbers gave you unto fame,
Lord of the lay, — I need not speak his name, —
Was one who felt; whose life was love or hate;
Born for extremes, he scorned the middle state,
And well he knew that, since the world began,
The heart was master in the world of man.

FIFTH OF NOVEMBER,

GUY FAWKES' DAY.

AT HOWE'S TAVERN, IN SUDBURY.

One fifth of November, when meadows were brown,
And the woods were all withered, — in Sudbury town
Four lads from the city, by special request,
At an old tavern met for a whole day of rest.

There was Henry and Austin and William and John,
And the glasses went round as the oak-wood went on,
And the spirit was kindly, the water was hot, —
Why then should Guy Fawkes and his day be forgot?

He was known in this tavern of old, I *expect*,
Though his name, like the turnpike, has come to neglect;
And I *guess* there was loyalty under this roof —
See! Her Majesty's picture remains for a proof.

But distinction is lost, — the Queen 's nobody now,
And a sovereign is not worth a sixpence to Howe,
Though his fathers before him, the sturdy old carles,
By the name of their monarch did christen the Charles.

There be names on the window-panes written with rings,
When the gentles wore diamonds and all was the king's;
When Joel and Hiram, as still they should do,
Served the punch, my dear Henry, to persons like you.

But the scutcheon is faded that hangs on the wall,
And the hearth looks forlorn in the desolate hall;
And the floor that has bent with the minuet's tread,
It is like a church-pavement — the dancers are dead.

Yet we summoned them back, and recalled ancient times,
And we roused the old Papist, repeating his rhymes,
And, to help on the humor, each man, with his drink,
Gave the arrantest rascal of whom he could think.

Well, we thought of all scandalous names that had been,
Cain, Catiline, Borgia, — the by-words of sin,
Saint Dominic Guzman, — Maràt, — Machiavèl, —
Some names that were whispered 't would start ye to tell.

Then Austin propounded — a health to old Nol!
And the Puritan rogues whom our speakers extol:
And John racked his brain for a villain of worth,
Till he happily lighted on Geordie the Fourth:

While Henry thus answered the jovial call,
Here 's to Louis Napoleon, the Prince of 'em all!
And William, to wind up the jest and the revel,
Said there 's none to cap him — so a health to the Devil!

But enough of rascality — now for a toast
To the most honest man Massachusetts can boast!
For his name — never mind — in this room he hath been,
And may only such guests come to Sudbury Inn!

ON SOME VERSES OF METASTASIO.*

WHAT man, by gift of any star,
  Deep-read in volumes deeply writ,
Rich in old knowledge, brought from far,
  On other's wisdom grafting his own wit,
  Or who, by any prosperous hit,
Can expound me what we are?
  What we are, have been, and may be —
  If man be full-grown man, — or but a baby?

What pale philosopher in glasses,
  Whose lectures Lowell overpaid for,

*FROM METASTASIO.

L' onda dal mar divisa
Bagna la valle e' l monte
Va passegiera
In fiume,
Va prigioniera
In fonte
Mormora sempre e geme
Fin che non torna al mar —
Al mar dov 'ella nacque
Dove acquisto gli umori
Dove da' lunghi errori
Spera di riposar.

Great man in genera and classes,
What clear-eyed genius, like Agassiz,
Can unfold what I was made for?

Tell me, learned commentator,
Critical on thy Creator,
In what act, or scene, or part,
Of life's tragic play, thou art —
What am I? king, clown, or what
Is our relation to the tangled plot?
And in what round of yon blue dome
Shall we, tired players, from the show come home?

For certes this is not our place,
Though for the moment we are here;
But, like the wild steed in the Roman race,
We are but seen, and for a space
Gleam in the Carnival — then disappear!
And the crowd closes on the courser's track,
And the Pope's blessing could not win him back!

Ev'n such a race is life indeed,
Rushing on in pride of speed,
Thorough vales — o'er mountain ridges —
Over deeps by frailest bridges —
(Gentle engineer, — take heed!)
Through dark woods and deserts dreary, —
Wastes that make remembrance weary, —
Whither! whither! ah! who knows?
Let us hope to some repose.

But we are bells that must be rung
Through all the changes, many times,

Until, in Heaven's high belfry hung,
  We sound the everlasting chimes;
And if we fail in this life's trial,
What can we look for but denial,
When the Great Judge declares our worth,
If of celestial metal, or of earth?

O, Science! canst thou give me aught
More definite, to clear my thought?
Naturalist! I ask of thee,
What am I — and what shall I be?
Say, am I now in some transition —
Red earth, or sandstone — what is my condition?
Was I a zoophyte at first?
  And shall I be an angel next?
Did I once crawl upon the sod?
  Answer — for knowledge I 'm athirst!
But with your learned terms perplext —
  May a poor worm grow up to be a god?

Say, born molluscous, do we then
Marble ourselves in time to men?
Until grief's rain-drops and the rust
Of many cares leave naught but dust?
  Tell me, philosopher, in few,
How 't was I hardened into coral!
  Ah! poets are as wise as you —
And this is Metastasio's moral.

Water, from its parent ocean
  Parted, never is content;
Ever murmuring, if in motion,
  Sullen, if in stillness pent:

Though it sparkle down the mountain,
  Laughing at the flowers it laves,
Leap in jet, or dance in fountain,
  Now in drops, and now in waves;

Still it murmurs as it flows,
  Still complaineth, till at last,
In the deep from which it rose,
  After all its wanderings past,
Sleeps the streamlet in repose.

www.ingramcontent.com/pod-product-compliance
Lightning Source LLC
LaVergne TN
LVHW011223110826
845150LV00006B/1520

* 9 7 8 1 4 2 5 5 1 5 8 2 9 *